CORN ISLAND RUNDOWN

CHIP HUNTER

This book is dedicated to my grandparents, Kit and George Lowman, who taught me that the world is not as large as many people think and that the word "No" can often mean "Maybe."

PREFACE

Rundown, also referred to as *Rondón* or *Fling Me Far,* is a stew from Jamaican and Tobago cuisine. Its main ingredients include fish, coconut milk, plantain, tomatoes, onions and seasoning.

Like Creole gumbo and other traditional recipes, the final product rests entirely in the hands of the chef, who is likely to serve it differently every time.

This book is a homemade stew based on fact, seasoned with a pinch of fiction. The recipe is inspired by a grand adventure I shared with my college classmate David Keeling, to whom I will always be grateful.

INTRODUCTION

Your journey will still be difficult, but the map shouldn't be! Knowing where you're going, how to get there, and how to tell where you are right now should be the easy part!

— BRIAN S. HOLMES

"Mon, I'm telling you… you won't ever leave Corn Island. And I just want you to remember that a Negro man once said…"

"…a Black man?" a traveler suggests.

"…that a Black man once said"—the ferry captain continues in his Caribbean croon—"…you would find your wife on Corn Island. Remember it, Mon. They have girls there from every nation. With blue and green eyes. And many with skin clearer than you."

Four men lean in around a wooden table crowded with bottles and empty plates. Jorge, captain of the *Fonseca*, which crosses the Gulfo de Fonseca from El Salvador to Nicaragua four times a day, waves to "Patron" for another round.

Dave Kipling and Chance Hooker, two travelers from the States, mop up smears of beef, rice, and frijoles with tortillas while Abe the Hitchhiker keeps the conversation limping along with idle hippie jabber; he has a saxophone and a bag of clothes at his feet.

Outside the open-air canteen *El Patio*, the water laps at orange-red sand. Pillars of jet-black rock guard the entrance to the harbor. At the bay's mouth, a stubby white lighthouse waits to fulfill its duty at dusk, and the clouds beyond the tropical forest mimic volcano smoke. A troop of grackles marches outside like noisy sentries, arguing over bits of food tossed their way.

Dave is in this Central American border town because he wants to be. Chance is here because he needs to be. For him, it is a temporary but vital escape.

The two unlikely companions, graduates of a traditionally all-men highbrow college, have been traveling for ten days. Caftan-clad Abe (a vagabond with no last name) has recently joined their travel team after thumbing a ride near Oaxaca, so now they are three.

Abe gained their gratitude at a local market, cutting prices for handcrafts in half by negotiating in broken Spanglish with enterprising entrepreneurs at every stall. He was often chased down the road by vendors sensing a cleverly bartered sale.

After that lesson, Dave drove and chatted eagerly with Abe as they rode with the windows down in Myrtle, the olive green 1968 Plymouth station wagon that had carried them all the way here from Lexington, Virginia. Dave quickly adopted much of the hippie hitchhiker's "far out" vernacular. Chance quietly rode "shotgun," watching a bronze-medal sun sink behind tree-covered hills as a stiff Pacific breeze blew east.

They arrived at the *Fonseca* dock too late for the ferry. The ticket booth was closed until morning (with no sign to indicate what time that would be), so the two travelers and Abe set out to find dinner.

Now they sit with Ferry Captain Jorge at the cantina, which caters to charter fishermen and long-distance travelers. The simple decor reminds Chance of how their trip started: over a pool game at a small college-town diner. There is no green felt tabletop in this place, but a jukebox tosses out country songs between Latino heartbreak ballads as they eat. More than three thousand miles from home, the basic fare and casual vibe feel somehow familiar.

A BOLD PLAN

One autumn day, among the speckled Blue Ridge Mountains, on the fringe of a small college town, Chance and Dave begin to forge a plan to set up a business far away.

Often called "Kip and Hook" and other times just "the Pirates," they kill hour upon hour sipping beer suds, poring over papers and maps, plotting a future together somewhere in the Caribbean. While other people are polishing academic resumes or prepping for pre-law exams, they convene nightly at a casual downtown hangout called The Paramount Inn, aka "the Mount."

They are an unlikely pair. Chance comes from Georgia and has curious blue eyes and a haywire hairdo covering his collar. Most nights he engages strangers with a slow Southern drawl. Dave speaks with an almost British-sounding accent, is somewhat aloof, and has an odd taste for ascots even when wearing shorts.

Each blends with the regular crowd of transient young men and local women mingling in high-backed booths, dining on burgers and beer, and placing quarters in lines on the green felt tables then waiting their turn to play pool. At closing time, the entrance to the Mount is locked and the blinds are drawn, but customers can finish a final glass while the owners clean up. Sometimes an extra pitcher or two is drawn after hours.

It's here on a night in early fall that Dave tells Chance about his plan to establish a fishing business in crystal Caribbean waters at a place called Corn Island. Dave invites Chance to join his team for this rare adventure. The offer comes at a good moment, just as Chance is holding his breath waiting for responses to several grad school applications in journalism. Dave wants to live where the weather is warm and wants a partner to get started on his future as a business tycoon.

"Why have I never heard of this place?" Chance asks one night after hours.

"It's a bit off the beaten path."

"How do you know about it?"

"Well, it's near my family home in Jamaica."

Dave knows his potential partner is currently just killing time, while he is more than ready to leave this tiny town and make his mark in the world. He makes the pitch more seriously after the diner has closed.

"...I tell you, there are so many lobster; you walk along the shore, reach down, and just pick them up. But those are the small ones, the easy ones. The real money is offshore."

"Sounds like a lot of work to me."

"It is work! But good exercise. And worth it."

"I'm sure. But what about the money? That's a long way from the market."

"I've got it all figured out. Just need a mate to go with me."

Pool balls click. The bald light bulbs hanging over the felt tables provide dim light. Pop, the owner, makes a final round gathering handfuls of glasses, then leans over a steaming metal sink and shouts, "Last call... for the last time."

Dave and Chance rise, leave the Mount together, and then part on the street, heading in opposite directions.

"Just got to get a wagon," shouts Dave.

"Let me think about it."

"Don't think too hard, mate. This train is leaving the station."

Chance marches up the brick sidewalk to his rustic retreat. Dave heads down the hill to his own.

At the top of a paved incline, Chance stops and looks at the old Campbell Hotel, a solid brick structure, the first wing of which he now owns. Built in 1809, it is recognized as a treasure by the National Trust for Historic Preservation and is currently under "restoration."

With no family or financial guidance, he purchased the property, converting most of a small family inheritance into this questionable real estate investment. After many sweaty months and smashed fingers, plus some blind luck, the property now pays for itself (and a little more) as a creaky home for college students. Chance lives mostly alone on the top floor.

Under a sparkling summer sky, he looks up from the street and sees a shadow passing behind thin curtains in his apartment. He walks around the historic, mostly empty building and enters from the back across a recently restored wooden porch.

Inside he crosses tongue-and-groove native pine floors, navigating by the streetlight reflected from the cracked plaster walls. The building's interior is nearly entirely a work in progress. Chance stops and looks around, absorbing its solid, historic strength, as he always does when entering the former home, hotel, and commercial building.

Tonight, he is quickly drawn back to the present by shuffling feet above. He climbs two flights of handcrafted stairs two steps at a time before entering his recently restored top floor suite with a mixture of eagerness and dread.

Mandy McCoy stands in the open kitchen preparing drinks and a meal. The open living quarters are ample but compact. Fire in a wood-burning stove is warming the room and casting a cozy glow on the sloped ceiling.

Just beyond the top of the stairs, the door leading to the bedroom and bathroom is closed. James Taylor moans and wails on an 8-track player. The square-shouldered woman with red hair, dressed in tight dungarees and a forest-plaid shirt, does not hear Chance enter. He watches her sway and wonders how he will introduce the topic he has kept secret for weeks.

"Hey girl. Been here long?"

Mandy turns and smiles. They move together and look into each other's eyes.

"Too long without you," she says. "I brought you dinner. Knew you'd need it."

"That's not all I need."

Later, they lie on Chance's quilted bed looking out at the night through rippled glass. Seasoned oak firewood has turned to embers in the stove. Relaxed and relieved, these two local misfits huddle together, against the cold more than anything else.

"I need to go soon."

"I know," Chance replies.

"No, I mean it. The last set ends at midnight... supposedly."

"Mmmm."

"I need to be home when he gets there. Really... well before."

"I know."

Moonlight spills across the room and draws swatches of pale shades across Mandy's form. She leans over Chance, her torso exposed like a statue across his chest.

As always, she looks, speaks, and behaves like no woman he has ever known. Eight years younger than her, Chance feels he is in the presence of a goddess.

They met two years ago, while he was a senior in college. Chance had just returned to a new life in the U.S. following a brief period of study abroad. His family, which was already splintered beyond repair, had finally shattered, leaving him homeless but self-sufficient by virtue of a modest trust fund, administered by a disinterested trustee.

When, at the age of twenty-one, he spent most of it on the hotel, he discovered an untapped affinity for historic buildings. He also met well-placed locals interested in seeing this neglected part of town revitalized. And he met Mandy, proprietress of an organic restaurant called Mama's Kitchen just across the street. He ate lunch there now and then and sometimes cooled off over a beer. After business hours, Mandy seemed to have time to burn.

They drifted together. She was drawn to his energy and boldness with his building. He was drawn by her tasty food and fluid motions behind the bar.

It was many weeks before he learned she was married.

Mandy's husband, Otis McCoy, is a distinguished professor lecturing on geography at Chance's college on the hill. A Navy vet with a Purple Heart, he taught himself to speak Greek and play the clawhammer banjo. He currently alternates between teaching classes in coffee shops by day and leading a string band at night.

Chance and Mandy now lie together, limbs entwined. Their evenings—and sometimes days—together nearly always end this way. A reluctance on her part to leave. A deep need to feel her beside him. They often talk about other "solutions."

"I don't know why I keep coming back to you. But I really need to go soon."

"I know."

"He finishes at midnight... supposedly."

"You know he never does."

"I need to be home when he gets there."

"I know, but there are always lots of encores. Particularly on Fridays."

"He wants to talk to you. Have you over for drinks and dinner."

"And maybe shoot me?"

"No... just get to know you."

"I don't want to be the cause of a family civil war."

"He's not like that."

"Funny. I already feel like a hostage."

As always, Mandy pushes her departure to the limit. She breaks away from their final kiss on the back porch and jogs across the gravel drive into the dark.

Chance watches Mandy disappear and suddenly remembers.

"I forgot to tell her... I'm leaving soon."

By early December, plans are set. Together, Chance and Dave buy a car, a 1968 Plymouth station wagon, which is instantly dubbed "Myrtle." Together, they load the vehicle with "necessary" equipment and, in a matter of days, the two adventurers put college life and the Blue Ridge Mountains behind them.

"We'll get whatever else we need along the way," Dave assures Chance.

"How do you know that?"

"Been there before."

"Oh, yeah."

Chance has confidence in Dave. Dave was born in Jamaica, as well as dressing and speaking like an aristocrat. Unlike Chance, Dave went to a fancy boarding school, but, most importantly, this is not his first trip to Nicaragua.

They stop over with friends along the way, first in Chance's hometown, Atlanta, then in Montgomery, Alabama, finally New Orleans. Along the way, Myrtle begins to show her age. Just outside New Orleans, Dave pulls the wagon over and demonstrates his mechanical ingenuity by correcting a minor muffler problem with a piece of baling wire. Chance is suitably impressed.

"Nice work."

"No big deal. Learned a lot keeping my old Triumph on the road. Pap had a handyman who lived nearby. Taught me a lot. Much more than my father did."

"Know what you mean. I learned more outside the home than in it. Changing tires. Hand tools. Stuff like that. Fact is... you're about to meet one of my mentors. Guy name Joe. He's taking us sailing in N'Awlins. He's a wizard with ropes and knots. An art teacher. Used to say, 'just try it.' Never heard that from my Dad."

During an overnight stay along the Gulf Coast, Joe treats Chance and Dave to lunch at the local yacht club, one of the oldest sailing retreats in the country. They sail beneath skirts of Spanish moss with lots of skiffs and other small boats on Lake Pontchartrain and fill their bellies with succulent shrimp.

Later, Laura Lee, another connection of a different sort, guides them down Bourbon Street. They feast on bright lights, oysters, and seafood gumbo. They are as impressed by the crowds wandering rues and alleys with cocktails in hand as they are by the iconic French Quarter architecture. Their evening ends camped out in Laura Lee's Uptown New Orleans living room floor.

The next morning, they continue west, lunching on red beans and rice in La Place, shopping for fishing tackle in Lafayette, and tightening one of Myrtle's front wheels with a lug wrench by the side of the road.

The travelers are mostly quiet as they take turns driving and riding.

Chance is thinking about college. He studied English because the works of Dickens, Eliot, and Hemingway were somewhat familiar and the classes were scheduled at reasonable times. Dave was a philosophy standout because the curriculum, like him, was daring and never absolute. There were always new paths to explore.

They rarely talk about college, as students with different majors who made friends in a different context. But occasionally they trade thoughts. Crossing the flatlands of Louisiana, Chance speaks up.

"So... what are you going to do with everything college taught you?"

"Try to be a respectable human. What about you, English major?"

"Absolutely clueless. I know nothing about engineering, science, math, or law. 'Bout all I can do is tell stories."

"Productive ones, I've noticed, particularly after a few..." says Dave with a wink.

Chance says nothing. He looks out at flat, barren cotton fields and thinks about Mandy. He hopes he hasn't wrecked her life. Their last night together was tense and inconclusive following his explanation of the planned trip to Corn Island. They had parted simply, by moonlight, with a light kiss. He had said, "I'll see you soon." And "I hope so," was all she had responded. It reminded Chance of an old black-and-white movie, maybe *Casablanca*, with a man and woman parting, possibly forever, but without an orchestrated score.

Now, the road buddies indulge in a massive steak dinner in Houston after the experienced traveler Dave argues that "… there's no telling when we'll have another decent meal."

This travel day ends at the forgettable Maria Motel in San Antonio, Texas, 550 miles from New Orleans.

CROSSING THE BORDER

The drive from San Antonio to the Mexican border consumes most of New Year's Eve. They celebrate their arrival in Laredo, Texas with soup and sandwiches in Mike's Bar and do a bit of provision gathering. Chance spends most of his time looking for an adapter to match a zoom lens for his camera, to no avail.

Back on the road, Chance scans Myrtle's radio dial for football games. He really doesn't care who's playing who, when or where, but does relish the traditional, seasonal sounds.

Crossing the Río Bravo, better known as the Rio Grande to the North, into Mexico is an anticlimactic tale of woe. They end up traversing the border three different times, two of which are by foot in the direction of the Aduana, the customs agents who pore over their passports, skeptically ask about their destination and purpose, and then inspect Myrtle multiple times.

Naturally, there is a problem with traveling with a weapon, even if it is "just a .22." It cannot be brought into Mexico. After a lengthy discussion, the travelers return to the U.S. in the company of Captain Davila, the Nuevo Laredo chief of police, who expedites the process of entry into the country with controlled cargo and announces that there will be a $17 charge for "through passage" of their vehicle. There is also a $9 "special tax." This turns out to be a "courtesy" charge for the procedure. Chance is livid. He finds this an outrage and refuses to pay the "special tax."

The two Americans are invited to take a seat on a nearby bench. Two hours later, they begin to see the merits of paying the tax and finally do so. The officials are now all smiles, and, once again, Dave and Chance are on their way. It is not clear whether the customs bureau or the beaming police chief benefits from this "special tax."

Next, the Mexican customs agent requests a paper they do not have related to the car. They must return to the U.S. again to secure the necessary documents for the car, and also one for the outboard motor lying like a corpse on Myrtle's back deck. After this last return journey, all the papers are finally acceptable.

The road to success is never smooth and clear. It is always under construction. You get stuck in massive traffic jams and sometimes fall into potholes.

They join the bustling traffic of Nuevo Laredo. It seems grimy and sleazy at first glance.

The impression is reinforced when they check in to the $6-per-night Sam's Hotel. Their much-anticipated arrival south of the border feels flat. Chance is silent and moody. Dave approves of the rate and pays up front with dollars. At last, their spirits are lifted as the long, frustrating day turns into Víspera de Año Nuevo, New Year's Eve.

There are hordes of people doing business on the street. Tour conductors pop up at every corner with special "deals" on guidance through the hidden secrets of the town. Novelty vendors point out woodenware on colorful blankets. The fragrance of roasted garlic fills the air. Sticks of grilled corn on the cob go for 25 cents. Blaring record shops lend a carnival air. Young boys with woven baskets direct traffic with whistles at busy intersections, stopping cars to offer Chiclets, the gum popular with kids in the States, which is even more prevalent in Mexico.

Dave leads Chance into a rowdy bar. Pushing through the crowd, they order tequila shots while making eye contact with deep-cleaved hustlers in dark corners. The two travelers try to persuade each other to make a move on a pair rolling their shoulders and pursing their lips but ultimately do nothing.

After toasting the New Year in a new country, they head back to Sam's Hotel.

On New Year's Day, Dave points Myrtle south on Mexico 85, and Chance looks out at miles and miles of cactus, donkeys, and Brahman cattle along the way. Orange trees shade thatched homes with small front yards. Men sporting cowboy hats (rather than sombreros) bend over neat lines of low-growing agave plants.

They pass through Monterrey and then stop for a lunch of frijoles con arroz in Linares. However, the gringos are more concerned about Myrtle's appetite for gas than the exotic food. They press on toward Ciudad Victoria as steep mountains give way to Galena Canyon. At an elevation of two hundred feet above sea level, it is lush with sugarcane and orange groves punctuating the occasional mud and clay homes.

Dave spends the afternoon in one of his quiet driving moods. Listening to the Orange Bowl on Myrtle's radio as the sun goes down makes Chance slightly wistful. It will be days before he learns that the undefeated Penn State Nittany Lions eventually beat LSU Tigers, 16 to 9. The delay and distance help put the event into the perspective of the broader world. Still, he feels a modest pang for home as they spend the night in Ciudad Victoria.

Despite lush, spectacular scenery, the next day's drive from Victoria to Ixmiquilpan (at an elevation more than five thousand feet), crossing the Tropic of Cancer, is grueling. They make slow progress through the gorgeous mountains. Myrtle groans a bit with the effort and once again drops her muffler.

Along the way, groups of locals huddle expectantly by the roadside in anticipation of the buses that drive the rough mountain highway with disconcerting abandon. Older adults and young boys commute to work carrying curved machetes. Women walk along well behind the men, many with shawls slung from their heads carrying firewood or solemn, well fed babies.

Stopping for gas along the route attracts barefoot children who gawk, giggle, and grunt at the strangers. Inside one small store, Dave buys sodas for the road, and Chance contributes crunchy snacks. The walls are plastered with pictures of national heroes, Emiliano Zapata and Pancho Villa. However, larger posters of Cantinflas show who the real boss is here.

BIG CITIES,
BRIGHT LIGHTS

O n day six of the journey, Chance and Dave drive through a dry area filled with rancheros. They continue through the Sierra Madre Oriental Mountains, growing comfortable with the rugged, rural vistas and the need to speak in pidgin Spanglish with lots of hand gestures at gas stations and roadside stands.

"Man, now this is the stuff I grew up with on television. *Lone Ranger. Zorro.* Bandits shooting guns on horseback, riding through the desert."

"I know what you mean," shouts back Dave. "But I didn't get much of that. My parents sent me back to England for school. Lots of black-and-white war movies."

"Too bad. Mine was all cowboys and Indians, like this."

Myrtle bears up well, only losing her muffler one more time on the road near Ciudad Valles. But Chance knows what to do now.

Entering Mexico City on a Friday is an eye-popping experience. Traffic is fierce, with a parade of headlights on the road, lights snaking their way down the street, cars hugging one another from bumper to bumper, exhaust fumes burping out, and traffic nose to tail all the way. The road becomes a giant parking lot, moving only inches at a time. The elegant colonial buildings are still decorated for the holidays. Dave directs Myrtle into the Polanco District, where there are many salutes to international literary figures.

A well-groomed woman with glistening black hair swept behind one ear, lavish lipstick, and dramatic eye makeup checks them in to the Hotel Polanco on Avenida Edgar Allan Poe. She informs the new arrivals in fluent English that there are many museums nearby. Her high heels click as she moves behind the desk.

"Is there a restaurant here?" Dave asks.

"Yes. And there are others nearby," she responds with only a pinch of accent. "I believe you will feel quite at home at Sir Winston Churchill's pub at the corner."

"I already do," Dave signals with a leer as they head for their room.

It has been close to a week without an American newspaper, so Chance buys an *LA Times* for an outrageous 60 cents. Scanning the paper on one of the beds with a view of the busy Avenida below sends him to sleep.

Later he walks the neighborhood, finds a barber, and gets a "severe" haircut, which costs about a buck and a half with tip. He returns to the room to find his partner examining his slicked-back hair in the bathroom mirror. Dave, the Jamaican with a British accent, fluffs the ascot at his throat and smooths wrinkles on a white dinner jacket Chance has not seen before.

"Ready for dinner? Maybe a drink before?" asks Dave.

"Yeah, I'm hungry."

"Let's check out a few of the desk lady's suggestions. Ready when you are."

Chance climbs into "his other jeans" and puts on his least

wilted shirt. Soon they are in Louie's Restaurant, which purports to be "the Most American in Town." And it may well be, as it is just a cut above a Shoney's. Here the wanderers ogle a few girls scattered around empty tables but don't speak to them.

"Let's walk around a bit. Take in a few sights."

"Could be dangerous," warns Chance. "We're probably just the kind of targets pros are looking for."

"You mean hookers?"

"Sure. And also pickpockets. This is Zona Rosa, right? Like the Red Light District in Amsterdam. And we couldn't look more out of place."

"Speak for yourself. But you may be right. Let's go back."

But Chance is wrong. Zona Rosa is posh, not seedy. Tasteful and historic. And the streetwalkers are all upscale. Taking a different route back to the hotel, they notice embassies and consulates flying lots of unfamiliar flags and pick up postcards to send home before turning in early for the night.

The tiring, twisting drive from Mexico City to Oaxaca takes them through arid terrain filled with twenty- to thirty-foot-tall cacti looking like armies of telephone poles or giant unlit candelabras.

They arrive in Oaxaca after 10 p.m. The gay, bright city immediately lifts their flagging spirits. They sip beer at an open-air cantina facing the main plaza, which is brightly decorated for the ongoing Navidad holiday. Finally, they call it a night in a $5 room with two beds and a private bath at the Rex Hotel.

The next day, they explore a large open-air market, gathering fruit for the drive. Out on the street, but not at a stall, Chance buys four fresh tangerines for a peso from a young mother who holds out the fruit for inspection but says nothing. He pretends not to notice that her breasts are bare. A plump baby watches the transaction while nursing with inquisitive chocolate eyes.

Oaxaca is a mecca for casual travelers, particularly the long-haired sort. Chance and Dave merge with other gringos dressed in colorful hippie travel garb as they inch through the fruit, vegetable, and knickknack stalls.

The local vendors are gentle but persistent. Youthful travelers like Chance and Dave are mostly outgoing, exuberantly greeting other "American" lookalikes with peace signs and "Right On"s. Soon their food basket is filled.

"OK," says Dave, "so much for Mexico, amigo. Time to hit the road again. On to Guatemala."

"Let's do this!"

They head south from Oaxaca, edging ever closer to the Pacific Ocean, through towns with colonial churches surrounded by stone walls, which allow them glimpses of snow-capped mountains in the distance.

In Tehuantepec they stop, grab street tacos, then continue south, admiring ranks of clay tile roofs, vestiges of the continental divide, and muscular clouds against a brilliant blue sky. Then, with some effort, they connect to the coastal road leading farther south through broad stretches of coffee plantations.

Crossing the border from Mexico into Guatemala only takes two hours and two total vehicle inspections. Pretty much as expected. But ten miles into Guatemala, progress comes to a complete stop.

"What the hell is going on up there?" says Dave.

Chance just shrugs.

"I'm going to go find out," says Dave.

They are sitting stalled in a long traffic line, mostly trucks loaded with sugarcane. Dave is eager to get on to their departure point for Corn Island, Bluefields, Nicaragua, which is hundreds of miles and a few more border crossings away.

Dave walks off into the brush to get a better view of what lies ahead. All he sees is an endless line of vehicles.

Commercial drivers climb out of cabs, one booted leg at a time. They smile and joke with each other, taking it all in their stride.

One driver descends to the road. Dave approaches him.

"*Hola, amigo. Que paso?*"

"Hello, gringo," says the trucker, squinting at Dave and pulling a half-smoked cheroot from his shirt. They both look down the road.

"Need a light?"

"Thanks."

"De nada."

"Can you see what's holding us up?"

"Naw. Doesn't matter. Will move when it moves," he says, taking a long pull.

A cop cruises by, waving drivers back into their vehicles, speaking in Spanish.

"What did he say?"

"Says the road should be clear in ten minutes."

"Oh, great. Got to go."

Dave lopes back to the car. The truck driver just laughs.

One hour later, fuming in the driver's seat, finally moving, Dave punches buttons on the radio and settles for some lively mariachi music, which only seems to make his mood darker.

"Sorry, I'm a bit contrary today," he says, and sighs.

The road slices through an area of thick vegetation. The day before, Chance had suffered from "Montezuma's revenge," but it passed reasonably quickly. Now he's relaxed, even complacent, relishing the endorphic comfort of recovery.

"Look at all the fruit," Chance chimes out.

"Yep. Grows like weeds here."

"Coconuts. Oranges. What are those pointy things?"

"Mangos. Or papayas."

"They're everywhere. And bananas! Look how they grow. Upside down. That's crazy."

"Yep. Bananas. And plantain. We have them back home, in Jamaica. But not quite *that* big."

For the rest of the day, they drive the western length of Guatemala. Dormant volcanoes protrude from the Sierra Madre mountains to Myrtle's left. To her right in the distance lies the broad Pacific Ocean. Just before dark, they arrive in Guatemala near the border with El Salvador. Here, in a town called Jutiapa, they find a small hotel attached to a family home.

A room with two beds at the Casa Regina costs two bucks. The common latrine is a hole in the ground behind a door with a latch. The owners are a jolly couple, glad to have this unexpected arrival. The husband speaks as much English as Dave does Spanish. The travelers are weary but attracted to a circus that has been set up in the plaza, one block away.

"Look at that. A good place to stretch our legs," says Dave.

"*No señors. Es más tarde.* Too late," the husband discourages them because it is time for bed and he must lock the door.

"Too bad. Looks like a postcard."

"Let's forget it. There'll be another down the road. Remember the last stop? Guy on a bike catching rings on his head? They're everywhere."

"You're right," Chance agrees.

The smiling owners lock the door, douse a couple of gas lights, and shuffle off to bed in slippers.

As Chance drifts off to sleep, he calculates the funds in his pack. He started at $450 and is already down to $300 after only ten days of travel. He lies there looking at the handcrafted rafters in the ceiling, listening to night sounds from the street, and wonders why he is here. He feels he is living someone else's life and yearns for his own. The responses to his applications for graduate studies are not due for another sixty days. He lies awake, wondering where he will be a year from now.

As day breaks, Dave and Chance are jolted awake by the cawing, flapping, and squawking of turkeys. It's a terrifying set of sounds. The young men rise quickly and leave in a hurry as though they are the ones under threat. No discussion. No washing. They can barely stand for the time it takes to pee in the primitive facilities, a concrete seat over a dark hole in the ground. In minutes, they are back on the road. They look to the plaza, and there is no tiny circus to be seen.

They continue south. Sugarcane fields of Guatemala give way to dense cotton and expansive banana groves in El Salvador. Dave is in an expansive mood and notes that "the end is now in sight."

Chance admires the lush scenery, including slow-moving young mothers and bare-bottomed babies, as Dave cruises down the open road. At midday, they stop for a lunch of roasted *pollo* in Acajutla, the largest seaport on the Salvadorean coast. They delay departure so that Chance can have his first dip in the Pacific. He walks across black, volcanic sand and finds the water much colder than expected.

Dave rearranges supplies in the wagon, distracting himself from his eagerness to press on.

Just before leaving Acajutla, Myrtle is stopped at an intersection. A group of young boys of scattered sizes and ages surround the car with baskets of Chiclets and buckets with soapy rags. In his blunt Spanish, Dave tells the gathering horde they don't want any snacks, and the car doesn't need a wash. Soon, though, the car is surrounded.

"*Gracias. No por favor...*"

"*Solo dos dólares.*"

"*Gracias... No!*"

"*Un dólar solamente...*"

"*No. Nada...*"

Dave eases his foot onto the accelerator and gently pushes forward. The youthful crowd moves with the car as if tied to the bumpers. Boys lean through the open windows, chattering like magpies. It's a Salvadorean version of a Mexican standoff.

As Myrtle slowly gains speed and pulls away, the enterprising street vendors drop off one by one and scoop up handfuls of mud, which they fling at the car.

Welcome to life on the street in El Salvador.

HITCHHIKER

The drive along the Pacific to La Libertad, El Salvador, is lovely. There is an elevated waterfront esplanade with a renovated 19th-century pier and fish market. Nearby, they stop for a lunch of raw oysters at a bar suitably called Oysteria, and then they test themselves against the strong surf.

As the afternoon dwindles, they drive past more dormant volcanoes with hardened dark lava flows, finally stopping at La Union on the shore of the Golfo de Fonseca. Moving to the edge of the gulf, they capture their first glimpse of Nicaragua far across the water.

"The Pacific. Smoking volcanoes. And a place called Nicaragua—just across that gulf."

"Amazing, right?"

"This is National Geographic gone 3D, 4D."

"Yep. But guess what."

"You're hungry."

"How'd you guess?"

At an open market, the adventurers conduct another sweep for food and supplies. They pick up hammocks and sleeping pads, which they stuff into Myrtle's crowded back end. While roaming the stalls, they meet another gringo wanderer with shaggy hair, a colorful caftan, and a well-worn leather pack.

Abraham Guttman—soon to be known as Abe the Hitch-hiker—is also heading south through Central America, but he has an open itinerary. They strike up a conversation, then follow him past vegetable stands, piles of colorful blankets, and wooden novelties. Abe demonstrates his bargaining skills with a leather craftsman. Appreciating his apparent fluency in vernacular Spanish, Dave offers Abe a ride through Honduras and into Nicaragua.

"Far out, man."

"Dinner first," says Dave.

"Solid," replies Abe.

Chance welcomes the arrival of a new conversation companion for Dave, having grown weary of this around-the-clock role. New pals Dave and Abe continue to cruise the market together. Chance strikes out on his own to find a place to cash a traveler's check but has no luck. However, he does find an inviting restaurant/bar called *El Patio*.

Soon the trio is sitting at a table in *El Patio* with Jorge, the ferry captain. Sipping beer, they listen to him speaking about Corn Island, Nicaragua, his home, and how much they will enjoy it there.

"Mon, I'm telling you… you won't ever leave Corn Island…"

The captain delivers a colorful profile of their ultimate destination in broken English while also keeping another conversation going in breezy Spanish with one lone, tottering drinker leaning at the bar. This balding man beams at Jorge while working his way through the room, sipping the remains of mostly empty glasses sitting here and there. This strange moment reminds Chance of a scene from a novel written by someone like Faulkner, in which they are characters frozen in time, surrounded by chatter in both English and Spanish.

Jorge offers Chance a raw turtle egg as he speaks. He shows Chance how to bite a small hole in an end of the leathery shell and then suck down the muck inside. It takes some force of will to down it. His companions watch with keen interest.

"How does it taste?"

"Not bad. Slimy. And chewy, at the same time. Could use some salt."

"Try another, amigo?" asks the ferry captain.

"Think I'll have my own plate. And another beer."

Soon a small plate with four more turtle eggs lands before Chance. He peels one, seasons the limp sac inside with salt, and eats the whole thing.

"Wow. That's a mouthful. Taste like chicken?"

Chance's eyes water, and he washes down the uncooked omelet with beer. He bats his eyes and sloshes back another gut-swilling splash of beer.

"Different."

He offers one to Dave, who pats his stomach and looks the other way, then holds out one to Abe.

"Thanks anyway. I'm vegetarian."

With another big day on the horizon, the travelers need a place to sleep. The air is warm—no clouds in the sky. The addition of free-spirited Abe inspires them to "rough it" and sleep outside.

"That should be no problem, man. Suits me," says Abe, clearly now feeling part of the group.

Since Myrtle is packed to the gills with supplies, the three travelers crowd onto the front bench seat. As they drive around the Golfo de Fonseca, Abe tells his story, and Dave welcomes the new conversation. Abe hails from New England and is a recent college dropout, which makes him roughly the same age as Dave and Chance.

He tells them that his days in a sixteen-story college dormitory looking out over a football field "...were so intense" that the academic and social regimentation drove him away. Instead, he chose to discover the world his way, "...through travel." He is a caricature of the '60s middle-class, privileged, pot-smoking, stoned-out hippie.

He has traveled frugally and craftily through Europe and North Africa. He speaks of many adventures along the way, including brushes with danger that make Chance glad to be traveling in a group, like having a sixteen-year-old travel partner raped in Morocco while the pair were recovering from dysentery in a hostel there, using more "...you know?"s and "like, like, like"s in his monologue than Chance has ever heard. He rattles on with sweeping generalizations about nothing in particular.

Still, Abe is a lively diversion. Soon both Dave and Chance find themselves unintentionally adopting his speech patterns, letting their own freak flags fly. Now a tightly bound gang of three, they drive through Honduras with no issue and arrive at the Nicaraguan border midafternoon. As usual, there are complications.

Here, soldiers with automatic weapons scowl and direct the trio to enter the security building. Inside, a large, sinister portrait of President Anastasio Somoza Debayle framed in matted rattan stares down at the uninvited visitors.

The "*Migración*" officer is dour. He speaks brusquely. It seems Dave's Jamaican passport is acceptable here since Jamaica is part of the British Commonwealth. Hitchhiker Abe knew how to purchase a tourist visa back in Honduras, so he is admitted after a few terse questions. Chance, as a U.S. citizen, must also have a visa though, but does not. He is directed to recross the border and acquire one.

Back in Honduras, they find the Nicaraguan consulate. A pale, shy woman carefully executes and issues a tourist visa (good for thirty days) and gives it to Chance. Meanwhile Dave and Abe walk the streets of Choluteca purchasing fresh fruit. Dave also finds a cooking pot with a lid and buys it—with Abe's assistance—at a discount.

They return to the border checkpoint, where their documents are inspected. There is also a cursory inspection of gear. The outboard motor receives careful attention. Dave's .22 rifle and ammunition get a shrug. This is the moment when Hippy-Dip Abe manages to talk down a $3 "car assessment" by handing a man in a worn official-looking shirt a few U.S. coins and blowing impromptu wails on his saxophone.

After what seems an eternity, Myrtle and passengers are waved on into Nicaragua with a grin. The portrait of Somoza scowls through a window.

Once again, they head south, guided by smoldering volcanoes. As darkness settles in, the travelers set up camp along the road in an inviting grove of trees near Chinandega.

Dave slings his hammock beneath some palms and climbs in. Chance pulls out his bedding and camps near Myrtle. Abe rolls out a thin pad and blanket several yards away and tootles "Good Night" by the Beatles on his sax. There is next to no traffic on the road, and they all fall deeply asleep beneath the brilliantly starlit sky.

The next day, they stay asleep until the sun is bright. Dave is up first and quickly disappears from view inside a dark thicket. Chance gazes up at a rapidly brightening blue sky. It reminds him of the Caribbean water he has seen in the Bahamas. He feels excited about new vistas in another new country now they are so close. Abe is last to wake. He stirs slowly, rooting through the bag by his head and greeting his new compadres with a grunt.

Dave checks oil and coolant levels in Myrtle. The van's age and health need to be kept in mind, so it is essential to tend to its first aid regularly.

Chance digs through the wagon's rear compartment, looking for groceries and a change of T-shirt. He shuffles gear around, compacting the load as best he can but with little improvement. The third rider makes Myrtle feel very small. Chance tries to make room for a passenger in the back seat, but this is impossible with the outboard motor hogging most of the rear compartment.

Dave and Chance are ready to roll. Abe's gear is tucked and folded where he slept. But there's no sight and no sound of their new third rider

"Must be taking a dump."

"Lucky guy. Wish I could."

"We'll have a big breakfast in Managua, then you'll be fine," says Dave. Sometimes he seems like the only adult on board.

Abe breaks out of the thicket after nearly fifteen minutes. He is bright and cheerful, not the grumpy guy who just left.

"'Bout time. Thought a jaguar had eaten you."

"No such luck. Sorry. Got a little congested."

"I was about to gather your remains."

Abe grins.

"No. We probably would have just identified them and moved on," offers Dave.

Abe looks to the sky and howls like an ape.

"Let's go. Got a boat to catch."

Abe fumbles with his pack, then rolls and re-rolls his sleeping pad. He tootles his sax before packing it away. He checks and rechecks his pockets. Then he pats them all and rechecks them again. Finally, he picks up his pack and his sax and heads to the car.

Dave is growing impatient behind the steering wheel. He races the engine a few times in a feeble effort to hurry things along. Chance opens the passenger door and holds it, gesturing for Abe to enter.

"Ah, man... the middle again?"

"You booked Economy class. Remember?"

Finally, they head out of the pine and palm grove and back onto the asphalt. It takes about a minute to figure out what Abe has been up to.

"I smell pot," says Dave in a loud, serious tone.

Chance sits quiet but alert.

"What? Where?"

"I smell pot! I've smoked enough. I know what it smells like."

"Well... I'll take some then," laughs Abe.

"Not funny."

"Oh, c'mon... dude!"

"You've been smoking. That's what took you so long just now. Which means... you had it on you coming through the border. You could have got us all busted."

Dave slams on the brakes, coming to a stop in the middle of the road. No vehicles are visible either way. A lone man leading a small train of mules heads toward them on the opposite side of the road.

"C'mon, man," says Abe. "We're in Central America, ya know. Where do you think it comes from?

"I don't care if we're in your shithouse in the Himalayas. You could have gotten us nabbed by the narcs. You fucked us over."

"Aww, man. It was barely enough for one joint, or I would have shared it."

"Get out."

"I can't believe this. It's everywhere."

"Not in this car. Get out—now!"

Chance listens to the exchange without saying a word,

knowing smoking pot is not the issue, but getting busted would be a huge problem. Dave pulls the wagon over and stops. Abe is out on the rocky side of the road in less than a minute, bag and sax in hand. Myrtle and everything she's brought (except for the marijuana-smoking hippie) quickly pull away.

Dave looks in the rearview mirror. He sees Abe already facing oncoming traffic with his thumb out. A truck filled with men standing in its flatbed motors by him without slowing down. Dave grits his teeth, then grins.

"Next stop, Managua."

But, inevitably, there is another stop on the way. About ten miles past the border, Myrtle blows a tire.

Again, the travelers pull over. They locate the spare (thankfully filled with air) and the jack. But no lug wrench. Fortunately, Dave's socket set works just fine.

But when it's time to lower Myrtle to the ground, the jack won't work. It went up fine; it just won't go down. Sometimes when things start falling apart, they just keep going that way. The partners try to lift "the old girl" but can't. They finally flag a truck and ask for help. One, then two trucks pull over to assist the gringos. It's a tandem team heading back home to Costa Rica.

The Americans still have no córdobas (nor colóns) to offer as a "gracias" gesture. But the truckers happily accept a couple of U.S. bucks and a few beers for their cooler. Everyone departs, waving and smiling broadly.

Chance's initial impression of Central Americans as warm, generous people is only deepened by the experience.

RUDE
AWAKENING

After a two-hour drive with Chance at the wheel, Myrtle makes it to Managua, Nicaragua, having passed the sacred town of El Viejo and the larger municipality Chinandega, former home to the modern poet Rubén Darío.

Coming out of the lush jungles of Guatemala, the scenic vistas of El Salvador's Pacific Coast, and the parade of Nicaragua's smoking volcanoes, their arrival in the capital city is grim and deflating.

With hands gripped firmly on the steering wheel, Chance remembers early talks about Central America over beers late at night and Dave speaking of volcanic eruptions. Back then, in the calm world of their little college town, smoking mountains seemed exciting, like something out of an adventure movie. What they see now is quite different. Managua is in ruins, apparently the aftermath of the most recent volcanic eruption over two years before.

As they enter the city, Myrtle and her passengers pass blocks and blocks of vacant buildings, finally making it to the heart of town. They see piles of stone and concrete rubble, windows without glass, and makeshift homes along every street. The heart of the capital of Nicaragua looks like a war zone. To a large degree, it is.

The ruling oligarch Somoza family has engaged in ideological, political, and open warfare with opposing factions here for decades. Political infighting is not the prime reason for the sad state of this historic spot, though. Some people call it greed.

Chance pulls up to the edge of Lago de Managua. He looks out across the broad lake, kills Myrtle's puttering engine, and is stunned by what he has just seen.

"Jeez... it's worse than I thought," Dave almost whispers.

"I can't believe it. We've come all this way... for this?"

"Well, it's really not what we're here for," Dave reminds them both.

For several minutes, Dave and Chance reflect on what they have seen. And now Chance slowly comprehends the level of violence nature has imposed on the city.

It is tragic to see how an entire historic city can be crushed in moments. And it becomes unspeakably pathetic when it happens more than once. The remains clearly speak of how the city would have looked before the earthquakes hit this place.

He imagined the scene. When the first earthquake begins, people freeze. Their brains fail to make sense of the messages that their ears and feet are sending. The ground starts moving, and the noise turns into thunder, made worse because the entire place starts vibrating. Then, at the speed of light, everyone starts moving for safety, running here and there, crushing whatever is under their feet. All of them, on autopilot, run for their lives. The walls roar and the floors scream; lights rapidly flicker before they die altogether. Finally, all that's left are abandoned buildings and mountains of rubble, crushing buildings, cars, furniture, and bodies under them.

"We need to find a place to stay."

"Here?"

"Got business here. Papers. Approvals. Always the papers."
Dave grits his teeth.

They drive slowly through the broken heart of the city. Police
monitor processions of vehicles, mostly painted in camouflage.
Uniformed soldiers watch the traffic flow at every corner. They
wear cartridge belts with stout batons and carry automatic
weapons. There are no working traffic lights. Police with whistles direct traffic, most of which is pedestrian. Myrtle seems
completely out of place.

At one stop, passenger Dave leans across Chance's chest and
asks a policeman about hotels in the area. The cop looks
annoyed. He grunts, points, and waves them away with furious
gestures.

When they finally manage to find Hotel Carlos V, it has seen
better days. Built in European style in the 1920s, the once
elegant façade now looks forlorn. French doors leading to small
terraces are boarded shut. Decorative finishes like finials and
balusters are missing, leaving only fractured bases like broken
teeth—a stairway leading from a small courtyard to the entrance
slopes in several different directions. Inside, the tall foyer smells
of decay, while the marble floor is cracked and uneven.

A small man rises behind a hand-carved front desk. He drops
a mustard-colored cat to the floor as a single incandescent bulb
hanging from a cast-iron chandelier casts dim light on his
balding head.

"*Buenos tardes*, dear sirs. May I help you with a room?"

Chance wonders how everyone knows to speak to them in
English. Is it their clothes? The way they walk? The jangle of
coins in their pockets?

It is helpful, but he also feels weird about it. He has become
conscious of how he looks and what it is that makes him
different to the residents of this place.

"*Sí. Tiene una camara para este noche?*"

"*Sí. Sí.* But of course, señor. Let me see." He turns his back and examines the keyboard.

"Ah... *Sí. Aquí.* Here, the best in the house. And for you is a special price."

Chance again marvels at how everything is "special" for them. Do they look like suckers? Or do they just act like it?

Dave negotiates with the chatty desk manager, who, after some hesitation, reaches up and grabs an antique key on a large wooden fob. Another short man with broad shoulders appears from nowhere. He wears a stained collarless jacket and offers to carry their bags. They decline.

Walking past two elevators, which are *"Fuera de service"* (Out of Service), they take the stairs to the third floor. With a bit of fanfare, the manager shows them a dreary room with two cots. It is muggy and moldy inside. A discolored mirror reflects a metal pitcher and basin occupying the top of a battered bureau. Their guide opens blinds on two glass doors leading to a small terrace. Here they have an elevated view of earthquake rubble and slow-moving traffic. Dave takes the key after inspecting a shared bathroom across the hall.

"Will señors be joining us for dinner?"

"No plans yet. You have a restaurant?"

"Of course, señor. Best in the barrio."

"Can I see a menu?"

"Ah. There is no need for a menu. Everything is fine—and fresh. Every day and night is different. I will speak with Cook."

Near dark, after tepid showers, the travel buddies are the only diners in the Carlos V dining room. Since there is no drapery or carpet, their voices bounce around the water-stained columns and parquet floor. The quiet man who offered to carry their bags is now their server and leads them to their table. The meal choice is simple. Chewy steak with beans and rice comes with or without grilled plantain.

After the meal, they set out for a walk outside to find cigars and get their bearings. There are very few lights. Carlos V has one wall-mounted lamp by the entrance. They head to the Hotel Intercontinental several blocks away down the Calle Rubén Darío on a plaza called Metrocentro.

Here, the vibe is entirely different. A crisply clad doorman (looking like the Philip Morris bellboy) welcomes them in English. American pop music drifts through the well-lit lobby.

At the adjoining bar, men with sports coats laugh and speak loudly over the din. Women in thigh-length skirts pose on barstools, smoke cigarettes, and sip martinis. The bartender makes eye contact as Chance and Dave enter and points to two vacant stools. He gives the counter a wipe and bobs his head, indicating he's ready for their order. Chance wonders if he will need to show an ID.

"Dos Carta Blancas, por favor," asks Dave.

Two foaming glasses arrive almost before Dave finishes his request. The wide-eyed travelers turn their backs to the bar, soak in the ambience, and feel almost at home. Each has another beer, then Dave asks for the check. The drinks cost more than their dinners, but they're worth it.

On the way out, a noisy American yells, "Watch your step."

Dave flashes a peace sign as they head out the door. They walk to the edge of the Intercontinental front entrance and look down the now pitch-dark paseo from which they came. The only lights come from the occasional car racing by. They discuss a walk back to their hotel and quickly chuck the idea. The cab ride costs the equivalent of two bucks but is worth it.

The desk manager, who appears to live beneath the keyboard, welcomes them back. The bag handler is also still here, sleeping in the shadows, chin on his chest. The new American guests approach to get the key. Neither is eager to return to their room.

"Will señors have a drink? Flor de Cana? Cerveza?"

"Two beers. How much?"

The manager scratches his chin, which seems to have grown a full beard since they left. Raising his eyes to the dark ceiling, he seeks guidance on today's price for beer. As he awaits inspiration, he strikes the pose of a scruffy saint.

Dave orders the beers once he hears they are less than half the cost of those at Hotel Intercon. Chance joins him for another round at a table with mismatched chairs in the lobby's brightest dim corner.

"We'll rise early tomorrow," Dave informs his partner.

"I agree."

"With any luck, we'll have papers in hand and be on our way to Rama by noon."

"Let's not jinx it."

Dave catches his partner's eye as he looks over Chance's shoulder. Chance turns to see the manager heading their way through the shadows with a bottle and three shot glasses.

"May I join the Dons?"

"Sure. Why not."

With the efficiency of a habitual action, the manager hooks sandaled toes beneath the seat of a chair from another table, turns it, then pushes it across the floor to the travelers' table. Sitting down in a smooth, practiced motion, he sets the glasses and half-drained bottle of Flor de Caña on the table.

"They call me '*El Loro*,' 'The Parrot.' It is because I see and hear, but remember nothing. It is why I have many friends. Amigo and amigas... *amigas*..." He emphasizes the last word and seems to be waiting for a familiar response.

"Hello, Parrot."

"*Buenos tardes, Loro.*"

"The Parrot" fills three glasses with cloudy rum. He raises one, salutes the two guests, and spills the liquid down his throat.

"*Desde mi familia a tu.*"

He encourages his new companions to do the same.

"*Desde mi familia. Sin cargo.* Please, drink. *Es gratis.* Free. No charge. From my family to you."

Hearing this, they knock them back. *El Loro* immediately pours another round. All join in.

"Now. What can I tell you? I have many young *amigas* who would like to meet you. They can be here in moments. Do you like dark hair? The fair hair? They are innocent. Not touched. Not like the ones you meet on the *calle*."

Dave listens, smiles, and twists in his chair. Chance is embarrassed and looks away. He examines the fluting on the columns and the enormous paintings on the walls. There are age-dimmed pastorals, portraits of proud men in stiff collars, swords in scabbards, and an elaborate coat of arms.

"Maybe you like the small young ones. Or I think you like the full ones. The ones with age?"

Chance looks into The Parrot's bottomless eyes as he waits for an answer.

"*Señor Loro*... can you tell me... who owns this hotel?"

The Parrot's expression changes dramatically. A protective distance drops down over his eyes. Where once a grizzled saint sat there now sits a solitary actor on an empty stage in a single spotlight.

"*Sí*... Yes... I can tell you."

"Is it your family?"

"No. Not anymore."

He begins the story of the hotel, The Parrot's family, the city of Managua, and Nicaragua.

"I have always lived here. In Managua. In this building. With thanks to my family.

"We are Tirados. We are proud. And very capable. Farmers and breeders. Already here when Managua became Nicaragua's capital in 1846.

"To be short, the British are always on the coast. But inland life is left to families. Families and the Church. Many descend from the Spanish, but local blood is strong. Like the Moskito."

The Parrot's eyes glaze. Dave and Chance stare to the bottom of their glasses. All three are wrapped in history and shadows.

"Families from León and Granada lay down disputes and unite. In Managua, the city grows, and so do families like Tirado. New homes. New business. We open doors to visitors. Soon we have hotels. My family creates this one. We call it Carlos V. Named for the King of Spain, no longer our enemy."

"I know this name," says Dave.

"Yes. A noble one. And so too Tirado. It is known across the country. For fine leather, belts, shoes, luggage. All hand tooled. Well made. Taking top price as far as Mexico City."

"Perhaps you will show me. I am looking for a scabbard. For a cutlass I wish to carry."

"With pleasure, amigo."

The three new friends salute each other with more rum.

"And so... the Tirado family lives happily forever?" asks Chance.

"No. We cannot say this. There have been many disappointments. One great one came before I was born. Once the canal that now goes through Panama was to come here. It would have been a great thing. But this did not happen."

The Parrot pauses to let this history lesson sink in.

"But time is a river. It rises and falls. Or maybe time is a wheel, spinning, bringing people, places, families like Tirado up and down.

"In 1931, when I was not yet a man, but ready to shoulder the world, it all came crumbling down. A great 'terramoto,' you call an earthquake, crushed us all. It wiped away this place, sending me and my family back to León. There we started again, learning lessons we never forget."

El Loro refills his shot glass, then knocks it back. He offers his audience of two another round. Dave pushes his glass forward while Chance covers his with his hand. *El Loro* drinks another in one smooth gulp. His eyes drift back again behind a frosty glaze.

"During my time growing up, there were many generals. Today too, there are many. Too many."

He drags three fingers beneath the table where they sit. He draws them back and shows Chance and Dave filthy dirt.

"You see this? This is what I live in today."

He talks about the rise of a general named Sandino and a family called Somoza. How these one-time allies within the Nicaraguan National Guard became rivals. He speaks of the rise of the resistance force called the Sandinista. And he describes a dynasty of dictators named Somoza. He recounts the cold-blooded murder of rebel leader Sandino by firing squad following a formal dinner at the Presidential Palace.

He elaborates on the assassination of the current president's father, Anastasio Somoza García, by a liberal poet. During three decades of Somoza leadership, the family has amassed a fortune estimated at $4 billion. The Parrot paints a bloody picture of a ruthless dictatorship.

"My country is a beautiful and dangerous place. *Cuidado, mes amigos.* Be careful. How you say...? Watch where you place your feet?"

"Watch your step?"

"*Sí.* Be careful with your steps."

The gringos settle their tab and head up for bed.

"Well, that was interesting. What do you think?" asks Chance, climbing the dim stairs.

"I think... I would not be telling any family secrets to someone with the nickname *Parrot*."

STREET TRAFFIC

Having stayed up late listening to The Parrot, Dave and Chance sleep in. It's Friday, their thirteenth day together on the road. They are expecting a busy one with bureaucrats, as they gather papers attesting to ownership of the car, the legality of their stay, and directions regarding necessary visas. As much as the day is expected to be busy and probably boring, the two are excited, as it will take them another big step closer to their future selves.

They grab a quick breakfast from the porter/server, who appears never to leave, just like *El Loro*. Then, looking beneath the cots one last time, each peers out the window at the noisy traffic below and leaves the room with no regret. Grabbing a couple of dusty bottles of water, Chance pays the room bill while Dave coaxes Myrtle from her overnight resting place.

The weather is clear and muggy, with watercolor-style pink clouds sailing east. It's barely mid-morning, and the temperature is already scorching. Sweat beads glow on Dave's forehead and upper lip.

"All set?"

"You bet. All good with Myrt?"

"Looks like. Needed a sip of oil. Seems she spent the night peacefully. No jimmied doors or windows."

They head out for Managua airport, which, according to the map, is nearby. But there are many detours and few direction signs. It takes an hour to drive twenty miles. They pull up to the no-nonsense airfield where small planes appear parked at random near the terminal. A few commercial ones are lined up across the runway. A thin stream of passengers with bags in hand makes its way to a twin-engine DC-3.

They go inside to ask for immigration assistance. The clerk points back to the door and indicates the process must begin with customs at "General de Aduana." They arrive at this office only to find that the man they need to see is at lunch and will not return until 2 p.m. So they go back to town to shop for a few more "necessities."

Chance as usual concentrates on postcards. Dave can feel the heat within his body. His warm fingers are pressed into his arms, digging as deep as they can. The veins are bulging in his forehead. He is suffering from anxiety about the customs process.

They return to "Aduana" before 2 p.m., but have to wait until 2:30 for the office to open. They spend the next two hours bouncing between Spanish and English, explaining the reason for their trip (to set up a fishing business on Corn Island), why they have all the gear in their possession (fishing tackle, an outboard motor, hand tools, and machetes), and why they really don't know how long they will be in Nicaragua.

Shoulder to shoulder, they fill out forms, display passports bearing stamps from several countries, and answer pointed questions as best as they can. They learn they can have a vehicle in Nicaragua for two weeks at no charge, but after that, it will cost the equivalent of 65 cents per day. There are others conducting business in the office, but none receive the attention they do. In fact, many locals seem to have gathered just to watch. At no time do uniformed officials seem pleased with their presence.

Dave is finally awarded a distinguished-looking paper, which seems to be the golden key to moving forward. He folds the thick document ceremoniously, places it near his heart, and pats it warmly. Chance has not seen Dave this happy the entire time they have been together.

"Let's go."

"That was painful! But somehow it feels good."

"Shhh. Now back to *Inmigración* and we're out of here."

They have no such luck. The immigration office is closed until 7 a.m. the next day, a Saturday. All the two can do is shrug and accept the way business is done here.

They find another simple room, close to the *Oficina Inmigración*, this time at the Hotel Colón. It is no improvement over the night before. The desk captain tells them that no hotel in Managua offers hot water as he shows them another shared bathroom.

"It is too warm here," their guide explains.

"I find that difficult to believe. What about the Intercontinental?" asks Chance. The captain just shrugs. Dave takes the key.

Given their current cash flow, they agree this is a good choice for the night. They discover the Shanghai Restaurant within walking distance and slurp down another indigenous Central American meal (arroz, frijoles, and an indeterminate meat) expertly prepared in an Asian kitchen. After dinner, they stroll through a well-stocked supermarket, where they purchase cigars, soap, pens, and more postcards.

Darkness closes in as they head back to the hotel. The sound of a noisy vehicle catches up with them from behind. A young man driving a battered Jeep crosses lanes and pulls up, matching his speed to theirs as they walk. It's hard to make out his words over the clattering engine. He shouts out to them. Dave shakes his head, shrugs his shoulders, and vigorously waves the driver away. Chance hears the word *"puta"* over and over. For a moment, it means nothing to him. Tires screech as the Jeep pulls away.

Soon another local approaches them. This time, it is a young woman, maybe just a girl, with a shawl, bright makeup, and tall heels. She stops beside a darkened doorway, lowers the shawl with one hand, and beckons with the other. There is no light on her face, but the primal invitation is quite clear. The two young travelers suddenly feel very immature. They pass quickly by the doorway and head straight for Hotel Colón.

IT'S A JUNGLE
OUT THERE

C hance wakes slowly.
 He lies on his cot, eyes closed, thinking, not sure if
Dave is still in the room or not. This is the most incredible
adventure of his life, and they are stuck bouncing like pinballs
between one stern official and another.

Their quest? Papers, bloody paperwork. The thought amuses
him. The pejorative word "bloody" has now infected his
thoughts, not just his speech. It is an indelible impression
created by his Jamaican travel partner, who often uses it.

Outside, he hears the constant groaning of large trucks.
Inside the room, there is only the mild whirring of a ceiling fan.

Today will be another day paddling through paperwork. They
should be sailing out on the high seas or dodging predators on
an exotic river. Instead, they are marching back and forth across
linoleum floors, passing from one concrete cell to another. Is
this what prison is like? At least in jail, someone else pays for
the meals. How does Dave put up with it all? Is his patience a

consequence of his family's British roots? Is this the much-ballyhooed "stiff upper lip"?

As though on cue, the door to their room swings open, banging against the wall. Chance rolls over and sees Dave poised at the threshold in a tight T-shirt, khaki shorts, and ankle-high boots, his hair slicked back. A superhero who has misplaced his cape, rosy skin glowing like pink champagne.

"Here now. Wake up. Read this."

Dave spins the front section of a week-old *Miami Herald* to the foot of Chance's cot. It's pointless pretending to be asleep, so Chance sits up.

"Read it. Quick. I told the guy at the desk I would bring it right back. It may explain why we're having so much trouble getting anything done. Hope to pull out in fifteen minutes. That bloody passport office opens at seven. And it's open for only half the day."

Stretching, Chance lets out a sleepy yawn, or groan. Lying on his back, he watches a fan stir the warm, wet air. He takes up the paper and sees the story, filling all of page two.

NICARAGUA WILL FREE 26 TO WIN HOSTAGE RELEASE

(MANAGUA, Nicaragua, Dec. 28)

The Nicaraguan government agreed today to release 26 political prisoners and fly them to Cuba in exchange for the lives of a group of prominent politicians and business leaders seized by leftist guerrillas at a Christmas party on Friday night.

It takes a long moment for Chance to get a grip on what he is seeing. Dave remains hyper-alert at the door.

"Is this for real?"

"Come on. Let's go. We'll get something to eat at the airport.

And… talk about that on the way."

"OK. Let me just finish this."

"Hurry up!"

The article reads like something out of a novel by Graham Greene. He rechecks the date: Sunday, the 29th, the same day they went to the yacht club in New Orleans, ate oysters and po'boys, and spent the night at Laura Lee's apartment. Why had they not heard about this? Chance reads on.

The drama began when the guerrillas burst into a private home at 7:15 p.m. Friday, killing three guards, and invaded a party given in honor of the United States Ambassador, Turner B. Shelton. But Mr. Shelton had left.

Chance and Dave had been far away on the road, heading toward Nicaragua, while the incident was underway. And it wasn't just a political standoff between disgruntled politicians, or a noisy demonstration by long-haired hipsters in groovy outfits. It was a bloody showdown. Just a few blocks from this hotel.

The party was held at the home of José Maria Castillo, a wealthy businessman and former Minister of Agriculture. As the intruders burst in, Mr. Castillo drew a gun and began firing. He was killed.

One hostage was a United States citizen, David Carpenter, 24 years old, a camera-shop manager from Rockville, Maryland, who is Mr. Castillo's son-in-law.

Only recently has Chance begun to follow international events. Now, suddenly, he is traveling through a country embroiled in conflict and confrontation. He and Dave have been driving Myrtle straight through the front line of a showdown between an entrenched autocratic government and an inspired opposition.

Dave leaves the room, his bag in hand.

As the siege wore on, President Anastasio Somoza Debayle, who had been in the United States at the time of the raid and hurried home, was said to have warned soldiers stationed around the house to do nothing that might provoke a gun battle.

Somoza has been in direct negotiation with the guerrillas by telephone on several occasions over the last two days.

Sitting on the edge of his cot in boxers and a cotton tee, Chance digs deep into his travel bag. He slathers himself with insect repellent, pulls on a pair of rip-proof trousers, slings a zippered pouch across his chest, then buttons a long-sleeve safari shirt. He steps into laceless boots, pockets a kerchief, then zips, then shoulders his travel bag. Grabbing the dog-eared *Miami Herald*, he leaves the room.

As Chance walks down the dark hall, he feels his gut tighten. He thinks about the twenty-four-year-old hostage David Carpenter, from Rockville, Maryland, who was caught up in the hostage incident.

Chance is the same age, twenty-four. His face tightens in a grim smile as he refrains from whistling a tune from the movie *The Wizard of Oz*. However, he does hear himself saying, "Well... you're not in Kansas anymore."

Crossing the lobby, Chance sees Myrtle at the hotel's front door. He leaves the room key and folded newspaper with a grinning clerk at the front desk. Outside, Dave peers eagerly into the lobby.

Chance tosses his bag through an open window, then climbs in. They are out of the bumpy drive and onto the street before the passenger door is fully shut.

There's plenty of foot traffic and many vendor carts with fruit, vegetables, and snacks. Women with large bags shop beneath tents that were not there the night before. Children run through parks and over cobblestones, inspecting trays of carved objects and sweets. Men with broad hats gather in the shade. Shoe shiners pop towels over gleaming boots.

It's Saturday in Managua.

The drive to the airport is short and direct. Mercifully, there is no line at the immigration office. But the hopeful travelers learn they must now report to the nearby police station for a "clean bill of health." This is bad news, but they put up no fight. Their time there exhausts the remainder of the morning and includes photos (front and side views), processed on-site. The results, with their grim expressions, would be suitable for wanted posters.

The police clear them just before noon. Returning to *Inmigración*, they learn that yet another photo session is required but that there is no time for it now because it is the midday meal break.

They are instructed to return at 2 p.m. It is the first time they have heard of this requirement. They are ushered out of the office as the clerk turns a sign on the door declaring the office is now *"Cerrado."*

Dave and Chance return to the car. They stare out at the quiet runway through Myrtle's streaked windshield. Heat rising from the tarmac makes palm trees quiver in the distance.

"This is nuts."

Dave does not respond. He narrows his gaze at the shimmering landscape.

"It's total crap. These people don't know what they're doing."

"Oh, they know what they're doing. They totally know what they're doing."

"They're jerking us off."

"Yep."

Chance spies a vendor with a cart beneath a faded tent. He leaves the car, slamming the door, and walks up to the curbside entrepreneur, a young man in his early teens with a dark complexion. He exchanges córdobas for two sausages wrapped in tortillas. They come with crisp plantain chips, which he drenches in green salsa. Walking back to the car, Chance balances the meal on a piece of wax paper.

"Here. I got two."

Still studying trees through the windshield, Dave turns, looks at Chance, says nothing, and then turns back to his private study of the landscape. At college, Dave earned a well-deserved reputation as an artist. He painted oils and acrylics of nearly every important building on the campus. He cultivated a following and joined with the alumni association to offer colored prints of the university's front lawn as rewards for generous donors. Chance wonders if, right now, his partner is composing an image in his mind for future reference.

"C'mon. Eat."

Dave just starts the engine. "We're leaving."

Chance licks his fingers, having inhaled one sausage dog. "Here. Eat this. I got it for you."

"We're leaving. If we come back at two, we'll just get the same fucking runaround. It's Saturday. They'll close early. And there won't be anyone here until Monday. We might get the bloody visa by the end of the business day, but probably not. Then it's Tuesday. Then there will be something else. It's rubbish. We're leaving."

"C'mon. Eat."

"This really is nuts," Dave says. "I've got no stomach for it. For that. For this. For none of this crap."

"You're the boss."

Myrtle sputters gravel high into the air as she leaves the airport permanently in her rearview mirror.

END OF THE ROAD

L eaving the airport in Managua also means leaving the relative sophistication of the Nicaraguan capital, the disruptive politics, and the streets piled with broken dreams. With Dave at the wheel, Chance sitting shotgun, and Myrtle doing all the real work, they head east toward Rama, Nicaragua, Bluefields, the Caribbean, and ultimately the Corn Islands. This leg of the trip puts the Pacific Ocean and the shrinking Sierra mountains well behind them.

Turning off the relatively reliable Pan-American Highway, Dave and Chance are expecting difficult passage, but they are pleasantly surprised. In spite of washouts, rocky spills, and other breaches in the road, they make good time.

Along the route, past mountains and dormant volcanoes, they pass through nameless pueblos and see rows upon rows of sugarcane and broad stretches of forest. They pass through the ancient city Juigalpa and a town called Villa Sandino without stopping, arriving at Rama on the banks of the Río Escondido mid-afternoon, well before dark.

The foliage is thick, a true jungle. Pulling up to the main dock at the river's edge is like stepping back in time. There is one primary wharf and many slips nearby with crooked posts for mooring lines jammed into the river's muddy bottom.

The wharf is a hive of human activity with nonstop loading and unloading of small boats. Stacks of plastic bags filled with fish are covered in ice. Men in ball caps push handcarts up a bouncing wooden ramp onto the ferry *Tachito*. Women in embroidered tops with bright floral patterns shuffle bulging bags or sit in groups shaded from the tropical sun. Young boys dart in and out like minnows. There is no place for a vehicle to park.

Dave heads away from the dock, then pulls Myrtle up to the front of Hotel Del Rio. He and Chance enter another quiet, shady lobby. The space is limited but feels spacious, thanks to a vaulted ceiling and wide-open windows. Clusters of inviting rattan chairs are empty. At the front desk, they ask an Asian man for a room for one night. He nods, finds a key, and, with hand gestures, invites them to follow.

The three walk down a narrow hall, stopping at a door with curved, hand-carved detail. The clerk opens it and stands aside. They enter a rustic room where a fan spins from glossy rafters, rising to a peaked thatch roof. The clerk opens shutters to a window that looks out on a wall of thick green leaves. Invisible birds chatter back and forth. Chance tries to identify a soothing floral fragrance. A spotless tiled bathroom adjoins the room with folded towels on a dark wooden counter and a basin with faucets. It's far better than either traveler expected.

They book the room, then step out onto the front porch. Two small, barefoot boys with jet-black hair are waiting to help with their bags. They speak an odd concoction of Spanish, English, and Creole patois. They handle the bags roughly but manage to get them to the room. Chance gives each boy a córdoba. The boys beam back their thanks and shove the coins into pockets in their dusty, baggy shorts.

The American travelers follow the boys back to the porch, where a neatly dressed woman with broad shoulders and dark hair peers into the crowd. A gathering of vendors, dockhands, and children, which has grown thicker since Dave and Chance first arrived, moves in crosscurrents near the wharf.

A group of boys about the ages of their bag handlers swiftly parades, single file, through the melee. Each holds a woven circle of reeds in both hands, rotating it left and right like a steering wheel. They drive imaginary vehicles through ferrymen and ferry riders as though driving a bus. Chance watches the snaky line of young boys and remembers how easy it was to amuse oneself not so long ago with a stick, a wheel, or a pile of stones.

"So there you are!" the woman says to the baggage-handling boys, then scolds them in rapid local terms. There is serious intent in her voice but not in her large, dark eyes. Her eyebrows arch high and her cheekbones and jaw stand out sharply. There is a hint of crimson on her lips above a pointed, dimpled chin.

The boys' bright expressions darken. Each looks up at the American travelers, shouts "gracias," then runs down the steps. They join other young boys on the dirt road.

The striking woman introduces herself as Esther, the boys' mother. She apologizes if the boys were rude.

"No, no, not at all. Quite helpful," Dave says. "Little gentlemen, actually. I'm Dave," he says, offering a handshake. She declines, arms crossed.

"And this is Chance, my mate." Chance nods. "We're here on a bit of an adventure."

"From Managua?"

"No. The U.S."

Dave speaks in broad terms about their quest. He has been to Corn Island before and knows about the abundant seafood there. He intends to establish a fishing business. They will trap langostinos to begin, then see what happens next. They have driven nearly three thousand miles to be here. But Rama is the end of the navigable road. Now, they must finish the final leg of this journey by water.

Chance stands by, looking out toward the pier, quietly allowing Dave to speak. There is an air of authority about the woman and yet her eyes are congenial, even inviting.

"We just need a boat."

"Really? That all sounds quite interesting. How big a boat do you need?" she asks.

"Large enough for the two of us. And—of course—loads of lobster. Then, in time, something larger. But right now we just need to get started. We already have the outboard," Dave beams.

Esther looks back out on the crowd. Her boys are gone, but she does not seem concerned.

"How do you plan to begin on the island? Do you have partners there?"

"No. This is my partner." He points to Chance, who says nothing but cocks his head.

"There are already lots of fishermen there. You may find competition."

"No problem. We're used to competition. I intend to buy the boat here in Rama. Take it down the river. Then hitch a ride out to Corn Island."

"Quite ambitious."

"Nothing ventured…"

A whistle from the ferry shrieks through the trees. The sound is deafening, causing the crowd on the dock to move more quickly in all directions.

Esther turns to watch the departure. Dave joins Chance leaning in on the porch rail. The final wooden cart rolls up the ramp and a deckhand draws it onto the ferry. Hand-waving on the boat and at the dock swells to a fury. More whistles blast and ship engines roar. Waves of water roll toward shore as the ferry backs away. Passengers and well-wishers squeal their goodbyes.

"I dread the day when they leave."

"Your boys? It won't be any time soon," Chance says.

"Too soon," she says, watching the ferry turn downstream.

The dockside crowd quickly thins. The ferry finds a strong downstream current and in minutes disappears around a grassy bend.

"I may be able to help you find a boat," says Esther without turning around.

"Really? Do tell me more," says Dave in a deepened voice.

"Oh boy," Chance thinks to himself, watching his partner assume a familiar role.

Two hours later, Myrtle, Dave, and Chance are heading north along the edge of the Río Escondido toward a small village called Esperanza just nine kilometers upstream from Rama. Esther has given them the name of a man who lives there with boats for sale. The two boys who helped with their bags at the hotel are in the back seat, leaning out the open windows like two well-behaved pets.

"*Esperanza*. What a perfect name," says Dave, slapping the map in his lap as he sits for once in the passenger seat.

"*Esperanza*. Did you know it means 'hope' in Spanish?"

"Well... no, I didn't," Chance looks up from the gravel road and over to Myrtle's side mirror. He sees a huge trail of dust following behind them, obscuring lush jungle on both sides of the road.

"...but I like the sound of it. We could use a little at this point. How much farther?"

"Hard to say. Not much detail on this map," Dave says.

The earlier conversation with Esther developed after a little more encouragement from Dave. She was born in Managua to an affluent, influential family. Her father is a former Foreign Service Officer under a previous Somoza regime. Her mother was raised in a family that still operates a successful import/export business. Esther is the only child. This makes her a "diplobrat" who got a lot of attention growing up.

Esther's father, Rolando Perez-Mora Debayle, served in several consular posts, including that of chargé d'affaires at the Nicaraguan Embassy in Washington, DC. During that time, Esther attended George Washington University near the Chancery, where the family lives. She met her future husband there, a pre-med student from North Carolina. She traveled often, both with and without her parents. In addition to old-school Spanish, she is fluent in English (with a smattering of French and German) and can convincingly converse with locals in Creole and the local Rama Indian dialect.

Now, barely thirty, she is mother of Rolando and Luis, the two boys. She manages and owns a timber company in Rama, part of a settlement from her divorce that provides a comfortable living.

"When in town..." she lives at the Hotel Del Rio. Esther declines to give the U.S. visitors her room number but assures them she has a "magnificent suite" just right for her "three-headed" family.

Rolando, the older of the two back seat boys, directs Chance down a bumpy dirt road, then on to a narrow two-lane gravel path surrounded by lush vegetation that seems to close behind the vehicle as they pass. Soon they see a wood plank house raised on piers made from tree trunks. There are covered porches in the front and back. The one to the rear is broad, with a sloping metal roof that faces the swirling brown river several meters below.

Chance pulls Myrtle into a pool of shade beneath palm trees

near the house. The boys leap out of the car before it has stopped. They run toward the house yelling.

"*Tío. Tío. Enrique. 'Rique. Tío.*"

A muscular man steps out of the house and onto the front porch. His skin is as weathered as stained leather. He wears an unbuttoned short-sleeve shirt, drooping shorts, a red ball cap with a St. Louis Cardinals logo, and no shoes.

Watching the boys race toward him, the man flashes a crooked grin. Luis arrives on the porch first. He is raised high above the man's head. Rolando wraps his arms around the man's middle and shuffles with him on the wooden floorboards as *Tío* Enrique spins round and round, holding little Luis near the ceiling.

"*Enrique. Hola Enrique! Yo soy David. Me llamo Dave.*"

"Yes? You have brought me my favorite nephews—*mis sobrinos*—*Luis y Rolando.* Señor, I thank you. And, I ask how can I help you?"

"Esther sent us."

"Ah. OK."

"We're looking for a boat," says Chance, impulsively.

"Ah. A boat. Small? *Grande?* Must it float?" Uncle 'Rique laughs at this old joke as he puts Luis down on the ground.

Soon they are standing on a narrow wooden pier jutting out into the swirling Río Escondido. Small boats are scattered all about. Most lie belly-up on the muddy bank. There are rowing boats, canoes, and pangas, all suited to navigate the Escondido. Some are painted. Others are weathered and treated only with a gleaming oil finish.

One of the larger ones catches Dave's eye. It is a twenty-foot-long dugout, carved completely from one massive tree trunk. Knife and chisel marks are apparent inside the craft. Wooden gunwales have been built up with planks along the sides. A flat transom in the stern could accommodate a gasoline motor. One small crack in the bow well above the waterline is patched with a tin can and putty.

As it bobs beside the creaking pier, moored fore and aft with rope as thick as human wrists, the weathered vessel looks sturdy and mature, as though it has traveled great distances with precious cargo. Unlike other boats nearby, it tosses and heaves like a restless thoroughbred confined in a stall. The name *Los Pumas* is hand-carved onto the starboard prow. There's a dignity about the dugout that belies its obvious age.

"What about this one, Señor Enrique?" Dave asks.

"So. My new Yankee friend has a keen eye."

"Jamaican," Dave corrects.

"Yes. Now I understand. Yes, that one is for sale."

"Can you bring it on land and turn it over? I'd like to take a look at the keel."

"Sure, Mon. Rolando, Luis. We need to take the boat out of the water and flip it over. Can you give me a hand? Can you take everything out?"

The boys nod and quickly climb into the boat. Water in the bilge rises above their ankles. Rolando removes boards covering a bait well. He pulls out a rusty coffee can and bails standing water from the bottom of the boat.

Luis reaches beneath the pilot seat at the transom and slowly turns to face the bow. He stands at attention with his arm straight out, holding the corpse of a rat the size of a boot by its tail.

SHOVING OFF

They stay longer in Esperanza than planned. Following a convincing inspection of the dugout, *Los Pumas*, Dave and *Tío* Enrique came to terms: one thousand córdobas for the vessel and two long-handled paddles. Roughly $140 seems like a good deal. In negotiations, Enrique remains firm on the price but sweetens the exchange by throwing in mooring lines, tin cans for bailing, and a box of fishing gear. Dave negotiates dockside delivery to Rama to arrive "early" the next day.

Enrique insists they celebrate their deal with dinner. As the late-afternoon sun sinks behind a cloud bank above broadleaf and conifer trees, Enrique's wife Marina tends the flames bouncing in a fire pit near the house. The men sit on squat tree stumps while the boys bounce up and down on a sagging wooden bench.

They dine on grilled fish, yucca, and plantain in the open air. There is also a steady flow of beer.

As the moon rises downstream above the Río Escondido, Dave, Chance, and the two boys ride back to Hotel Del Rio.

Rolando, the older of the two boys, who is in Myrtle's passenger seat, points the way. Chance and Luis crowd together on the rear seat. Through the open window, they watch silhouettes of tropical plants that look like animated cartoons in the night. The soft breeze blowing through the car is warm, humid, and pleasant; it has everyone thinking of bed.

Back at the hotel, the gringos pack and repack personal gear.

"What time tomorrow should we expect *Tío?*" asks Chance, rolling T-shirts and socks.

"He said 'early.'"

"I heard. But what does that mean? Nobody here wears a watch. There are no clocks on the walls."

"We'll find out tomorrow. We're just three hours upstream from Bluefields, according to the guy at the desk."

"You've been there before, right?"

"Yeah."

"You know a hotel?"

"There are a few. That won't be a problem. It's a port town. Lots of friendly hostesses, if you know what I mean."

"Right. Bunks by the hour?"

"Something like that. Ready to turn in?"

"Already there."

Dave twists the knob on the kerosene lamp, dousing its flame. Chance guesses it's about 10 p.m. There's still plenty of noise on the street. Chance jots a few notes in his day book by moonlight. Today is definitely one to remember. Tomorrow will likely be the same. The image of Esther leaning across the porch rail looking out at a busy world lulls him to sleep.

Parallel fingers of morning light pry their way through a window. Chance wakes slowly to the sounds of purring motorcycles and shuffling feet on paving stones.

Quietly, he grabs his camera and leaves the room. Creaky floorboards are the only sound in the hotel as he walks down the hall. No one is at the front desk. And no one is in the lobby. Stepping out onto the street, he is absorbed by a thick cloud of mist.

Vague human forms pass by, some in a rush. They are featureless, more shadow than substance. Voices and traffic noise are muffled by the fog. A muddy brown dog sniffs his pant cuff then vanishes into the vapor. Chance has never seen fog this thick. Bicycles with tightly filled baskets are visible only for moments. Traffic moves only toward the river.

Today, a different ferry is tied at the dock. Small boats paddle and pole beside it, like bees swarming a nest. One at a time, dugouts, pangas, and small rafts pull up to the ferry. Men and women, many with babies, hand up items to open hands then fade back into the fog.

Chance feels as if he is an intruder in someone else's dream. A huge parrot watches him from a tree at the river's edge. The bird's eyes bulge as Chance snaps one picture, then another, and another. The bird and the young American seem to be the only observers of the bustling scene. Everyone else is consumed with important chores.

When Chance returns to the hotel, Dave is coming down the front steps, bag in hand.

"Morning. Did you see him yet?"

"Nope. Not him nor the dugout. Actually, pretty hard to see anything. Walked all along the pier. Never saw a thicker fog."

"It'll burn off. It's like this often."

"You don't think Uncle Enrique—*Tío*—would stiff us, do you?"

"Naw. Wants the rest of his cords. He'll be here. Said 'early.' Could be nine or could be noon. Bloody hard thing about these river people. They time things by the boats. Did you eat?"

"Not yet. You?"

"Naw. Didn't see anybody in the dining room. Guess we're on our own."

"I think it's Sunday. Maybe everybody's off."

As if on cue, a chapel bell rings. Dave pauses and listens. Chimes strike seven times then stop.

"Guess it's seven. I figure we've got some time. See anything down by the pier?"

"Couple of carts. Lots of people. And I thought I was an early riser."

"They're all trying to beat the heat. And the bugs. Let's go see what we can find. But we'll check the car first."

They walk behind the hotel to where Myrtle is parked. Dave gives the wagon a once-over and concludes "all is good." He unlocks the rear, reorganizes a bit, finds room for his bag, and slams the door shut. Chance watches the mist begin to lift. They wander up and down the wharf, where they find a cart with tacos but decide to wait.

They buy juice and fish in tins at the Chinese general store. Dave examines fishing gear. Chance asks about postcards, but there are none.

They return to the wharf, this time with Myrtle. The melee of passengers, bags, and carts has picked up speed. Arrangements have been made for an extended stay for their wagon behind the hotel. Dave assures the owner they will be back "soon." The owner assures Dave he will keep an eye on Myrtle for a small fee and a promise of more overnight stays when the travelers return. Now their slightly fickle wagon is sitting quietly with all her doors open.

Dave has had plenty of time to inspect their possessions. Everything is neatly arranged and ready for transportation from *Los Pumas* to Bluefields and then on to Corn Island. Dave scans the river upstream every five or ten minutes. Chance finds a shady spot. With his bedroll behind his head, he reads, makes notes in his journal, then naps like a local.

Neither Dave nor Chance is sure about the time of day, even though Dave has finally put on the treasured, spring-wound, waterproof Timex he's so far kept in his bag.

"Don't want to be a moving target..." he explained in Managua. "...belonged to my Grand in the War."

Time is a luxury here. A thing to enjoy, not to serve. Dave sets his watch to the chimes of the little Catholic cathedral in the plaza. But who knows how those bells are set?

Still, it's clearly no longer morning. Church attendees have come and gone from strolls by the wharf. The party boys from the night before are again propped on porches, sipping bottles. It's probably "early" afternoon. And this may be the "early" Tío meant when predicting his arrival.

Being from the languid islands of coastal Georgia, Chance understands the fluidity of time and has a naturally casual attitude toward appointments. Dave is a different animal. Time is important. It is "dear" to him.

So, the Jamaican spends much of the morning rearranging travel gear, inspecting and securing bundles, looking slightly exasperated.

It takes a bit of persuasion to urge Dave back to the hotel, but he agrees when Chance mentions he thinks he can see Esther and her boys sitting where she was the night before. After a quick final check of the gear, they join Esther for a casual buffet on the porch, a major step up from tacos in carts at the wharf.

The grown-ups load up on mango, tortillas, and dark coffee. The boys prefer dry cereal from cardboard boxes with milk. Dave beams at the attention Esther directs his way.

"I can't thank you enough for helping us find a boat and seeing to it that Tío gets back upriver today. And... for allowing the boys to join us."

"A pleasure, I assure you, for him, the boys... and me."

"And we look forward to reconnecting when we return."

"Oh. So, you're already planning to leave the island even before you get there?"

Chance smirks at Esther's coy handling of his opportunistic partner. He appreciates the way she treats the gringos like slightly older versions of her own boys.

After the second cup of coffee, Dave can no longer conceal his eagerness to depart. They all walk down to the wharf and, a few minutes later, *Tío* pulls up, poling *Los Pumas* from the rapid downstream current to calmer waters by the wharf. He has drifted the entire way with the downstream current. When he sees them gathered dockside, he stands, gives a broad sweep with his hat, then poles rapidly toward shore. Dave is like a puppy on a leash. If there were a long enough line, he would clearly pull the boat to the dock by himself.

"*Hola mis amigos...*"

"*Hola, hola. Rapido. El tiempo... el tiempo se desvanece. Rapido. Rapido. Prisa. Prisa.*"

"*Sí. Sí.*"

The two boys jump in the boat before *Tío* has time to make it fast. They swarm their uncle. He wraps arms around them both. Chance secures the boat to the dock as Dave and *Tío* retreat into the shade to conclude their transaction. Returning to the dock, both are evidently satisfied.

In little more than an hour, the loaded dugout shoves off. It takes all three men to mount the outboard motor that has defied the odds and made it all the way from Virginia. It fits on the transom surprisingly well. Dave and *Tío* tinker with placement, connect the fuel line, and prime the pump. Dave pulls the starter cord. Nothing. He pulls again and again, but there's only the sound of his grunting and the recoiling of the cord. Once more, no ignition.

Tío leans in. He takes the cord and pulls it just as Dave has done. Nothing. He examines the motor and makes a small adjustment. This time the motor rumbles. Another small adjustment and another determined pull. The motor shimmers, rumbles, and then roars to life. *Tío* makes one final adjustment. The motor purrs in the water.

Esther, *Tío*, and the boys wave *adios* and wish the gringos *"Buena suerte."* Chance would actually like to stay another day.

An hour downriver, Chance recalls it's Super Bowl Sunday. He thinks this one will be particularly important because he will not be at a friend's house, sunk into a couch watching the National Football League's championship game, guzzling beer, and eating crunchy things.

Instead, he is floating down the Río Escondido, the "Hidden River," in a Latin American country he would have had trouble locating in an atlas at the time of last year's Super Bowl game. He tries to remember the winner of that game, or even who played, but he can't. It all seems so far away. He does however remember watching the game with Mandy, under the covers at the drafty Campbell Hotel.

This year he is in a hand-carved canoe with a relatively new friend heading for the Caribbean Sea. He looks out at lush jungle farmland, where gentle Brahman cattle graze behind twisted rail fences. The massive bulls look ferocious and females with long, floppy ears gently graze beside flocks of ivory white cranes.

He would not trade this splintered seat on a small boat in Nicaragua for a private box on the fifty-yard line wherever this year's Super Bowl is being played.

"Big game day today back in the States. Best of the best playing in the Super Bowl."

"Super Bore, if you ask me," shouts back Dave over the motor.

"Depends on who you're with."

63

"I guess that's right."

They have been on the river for about an hour, taking advantage of the downstream current by staying in its center. The river is dark but clear, like coffee without cream. Occasional plank and thatch huts, many on stilts, punctuate the dense backdrop of coconut and palms, mahogany, breadnut, and cottonwood trees. Many shrubs are blossoming despite it being the dry season in the second week of January.

Traffic on the river is evenly distributed between dugout and speedboat. *Los Pumas* is powered by the Johnson 40 outboard motor, which sits a bit high on the transom. Dave assures Chance they will correct this "…on the island." At this moment, it is their most valuable asset.

At this point, the river is about a quarter of a mile wide. Dave tends to the motor like a proud parent. Chance is charged with watching out for obstructions ahead. The task is undemanding, so he takes out his logbook, settles back, and makes a few notes.

"Watch it! What's that…? Heads up, man. You're the lookout! That's what you're there for!"

Dave diverts sharply to the left. They barely miss a huge tree limb floating just beneath the surface. A water bird rises slowly as they pass by and disappears into the trees. Chance puts his book away and leans sharply forward. There is no further talk for a long time.

Afternoon fades into evening. The first of two six-gallon gas tanks is now empty. They hail a noisy powerboat skittering by. The boat slows, turns, and then motors back upstream. Pulling up to *Los Pumas*, the lone fisherman reaches out, grabs a gunwale on the dugout, and lets his motor idle.

Dave salutes the local in an affected-sounding, singsong dialect. Chance can barely make out what the two discuss. It seems that Mahogany Creek, where they are now idling, is about halfway to their destination, Bluefields. There is no gas between here and there. In fact, there is no gas for sale in Blue-fields. One must cross the bay to El Bluff to fill up.

Dave absorbs the information. There is a nervous twitch in his eye. The grizzled fisherman, now standing in his rocking canoe, recommends they "flag a ship" passing by for gas or a tow. He cannot offer any because he is nearly empty and is leaving the river for his home just past the next bend. Chance would like to document the encounter with a photo, but he resists the urge.

Looking beyond them at the setting sun, the local wishes the English-speaking paddlers *"Buena suerte,"* pushes off from their boat, and departs. At that very moment, their "good luck" appears upstream even before the fisherman disappears behind tall grass.

The *Carmelita G.* gives the stalled gringos a toot. It is a small freighter with two open decks. Smoke from its stack continues downstream even as the vessel slows down. A sturdy deckhand in baggy shorts waves vigorously and gestures for Dave and Chance to paddle to the vessel.

"Head that way," Chance suggests.

Priming the fuel pump, Dave wakes the motor and points their dugout's prow toward the nearest downstream bend. With luck, they will catch up with the larger vessel there. Chance paddles as hard as he can. In a short time, although it seems longer, it works. The grinning deckhand tosses a rope. Chance grabs it like a survivor of the *Titanic*, stands up, and then pulls *Los Pumas* alongside the *Carmelita G.* He makes the line fast at the bow. The deckhand throws another line to Dave, who wraps the rope around a wooden cleat. Dozens of passengers watch from the decks.

The deckhand ties the line on his end and helps the two stranded sailors aboard. He grins broadly. The freighter now shifts engine thrust forward and they pick up speed, heading toward the coast. Standing about five feet tall on bare splayed feet, Jacob Palmerston speaks in rapid bursts.

"Name's Jacob. But the crew calls me Cookie 'cuz I do more than just tie ropes."

"Good English there, Cookie. Thanks for helping us out. I'm Dave. This is Chance. Been to the U.S.?"

"Been lots of places. States. Mexico. Cuba. Speak a few languages. Spanish. Some English. And some you never heard before."

Dave looks at Chance.

"How much for the lift?"

"How about 30 cords, Bossman?"

"You got a deal."

Jacob secures *Los Pumas* to the stern, where it calmly bobs in the *Carmelita*'s wake. Then Jacob takes the gringos up top to meet "El Skipper." Dave and Chance enter the noisy bridge and introduce themselves.

Keeping one hand on the wheel and an eye on the river ahead, the helmsman introduces himself as "Captain." Dave and Captain converse in what sounds like Jamaican, while Chance watches a crew member on the foredeck waving a large flashlight back and forth over the now dark river ahead. There are cooking fires on either bank.

They arrive in Bluefields about midnight. A single light on a pole shines down on tall men in T-shirts milling about, some with wooden wheelbarrows.

Jacob Palmerston bounces onto the boat dock from below and tosses lines onto the dock. The *Carmelita G.* engine roars as it is jammed into reverse. Anonymous hands pull at ropes and tighten them on wooden cleats. Passengers gather on the shore side of the boat and it lists a bit. Two long-armed men latch the exit ramp into place. Now men, women, and sleepy children, all with bags in hand or on shoulders, disembark.

Dave talks to Jacob on the dock.

"Can we leave our gear on board for the night?"

"No problem. Go check out 'Mama's' if you need a place to stay. Tell the guy at the door Cookie Sent you."

"Sure he won't jack up the rate?"

"Depends on what you ask for," Jacob chuckles and waddles away.

Chance follows Dave down a dark street, past quiet stucco and wood frame buildings. They enter one with no sign and speak with a man at a cracked door. They each pay ten córdobas for a bunk and access to a shower.

Whereas Chance is exhausted, Dave is energized. He immediately goes out to find something to eat and to check on the mooring of *Los Pumas*. Meanwhile Chance melts onto the thin bed.

Within minutes, he is fighting bedbugs. He tries to ignore them for an hour or more but finally throws off the mattress and, using his own blanket, falls asleep on bare springs.

HOME PORT FOR PIRATES

B ags in hand, the two adventurers step out into the bright morning. They have made it to the port town, once recognized as capital of the Mosquito Coast. Now only Bahía de Bluefields separates Chance and Dave from their next destination, El Bluff (also known as Blufftton) on Nicaragua's Caribbean coast.

The town looks entirely different than it did the night before. There are pastel stucco buildings, some with thatched roofs, vendors at outdoor stalls, and hand-painted signs in contrasting colors. There is an open-air fish market, a Catholic church, palm trees, taxi cabs, and motorbikes. People mill about wearing sandals and straw hats. The new arrivals walk toward the center of town and grab food from the first cart they see.

They hear unfamiliar strains of syncopated drums and guitars. It's jazzy and soulful at the same time. Chance learns later that this music pouring from nearly every open door is called reggae. It's a far cry from the psychedelic pop flooding in from Europe and the Motown sounds Chance grows up on in the U.S.

Back at the dock, *Los Pumas* bobs beside the *Carmelita* as though it is eager to embark. The passenger boat where their gear is stowed shares space with commercial vessels and looks much smaller than Chance remembers.

As promised, Jacob has done a good job securing their twenty-foot canoe. It takes about half an hour to reload gear into the dugout and secure it beneath a tarp with cord. For once, Chance has the advantage. He's good with knots, and Dave approves the final stowage. With a little tinkering, the Johnson 40 outboard cranks up. Chance slips lines away from the cleats. They pull out into Bahía and toward the now fully risen sun.

"So where are all the blue fields?" Chance shouts.

"Aren't any. There may be a few up on those hills. But this is more of a fishing town."

"So why the name? Hopeful, I guess."

"Named after a pirate... something like Blaufelt... from Europe, maybe a German—or Dutch—a long time ago. This was always known as a safe port for buccaneers. They hung out here between raids, made babies, way back when. A hundred years ago. Probably more. They'd jump ships of all kinds going up and down the Mosquito Coast. Still do."

The chopping of the sea gets heavier. Dave gives the pump on the fuel line a squeeze, then cranks the motor wide open. The veteran road trippers, now rookie seamen, look hard at low-lying land on the horizon.

"What do you mean 'still' do?" Chance yells back at Dave.

"Pirates still own these waters. Cargo's just a little different. Coke mostly. Not much of a market for slaves anymore. At least, not the Jamaican nor African kind."

"Coke? Cocaine?"

"You got it, mate. Bluefield's a major port of entry. Sometimes importers race up near shore, do a one-eighty, cut it loose, then speed away. Coke and pot. The tide washes bundles up onto the beach. Then a 'receiver' picks it up. It's big business here."

"How do they get away with it?"

"Well... like I say, it's a big part of the economy. Also, you know... out of sight, out of mind. Why do you think they call that river we just came down 'Hidden River'?"

"Río Escondido?"

"Yeah. Or as I prefer to interpret it, 'Lost River.'"

Heat from the sun warms Chance's face as Dave bounces *Los Pumas* across the waves. They steady themselves by leaning into the chop and gripping the rails. Chance reflects on the million-dollar hostage showdown in Managua he read about as they cruise in a hand-carved canoe through a major cocaine-smuggling point of entry.

He looks back at Dave, aviator shades reflecting the morning sun, teeth gritted, firm hand on the tiller, sea spray gleaming on his bristly chin. The Jamaican looks like he has been cast for this role.

And Chance asks himself, "What have I gotten myself into?"

They make dock at El Bluff after a forty-five-minute crossing, during the height of the morning rush. The wharf is much higher here than at Bluefields. Everything seems bigger and stranger. As the sun climbs toward noon, Dave directs Chance to stay by the boat while he searches for petrol, a place for lunch, and a tow. They have discussed striking out on their own across seventy nautical miles to Corn Island but are talked out of it by various locals. Their dugout catches the eyes of seasoned seamen and attracts favorable comments. Chance begins to feel at home on these strange docks.

Sitting in the sun with no shade, Chance grows hot. He's tempted to take a dip in the water but is put off by its oily sheen. There is a steady clamor of banging metal. Forklifts cruise the elevated dock above his head. Occasional voices shout

out directions and greetings in Creole English, which still sounds foreign to him.

Over and over, he checks the tautness of knots on their mooring lines and those on their load. He also checks the fuel tanks. One is about half full. The other is empty.

Without thinking much about it, he grabs a coffee can and bails the bottom of *Los Pumas*. He recently learned that the boat's name translates in English to "The Cougars" but at this point in their journey, Chance feels more like a stray cat than a cougar.

He checks for his passport for the fiftieth time that day in its pouch beneath his open collar shirt. He pats the wallet in his cargo shorts, takes it out, and opens it. He sees the shortlist of emergency telephone numbers there: his father, his sister, and Mandy, his sometimes girlfriend back home. There is no memento of Mandy. He counts his cash. There are four hundred córdobas (about $50) and one U.S. $20 bill tucked inside the wallet's leather lining. This hiding place would take nimble, larcenous fingers about two seconds to discover. There are also American Express traveler's checks tucked in the lining of his rucksack.

After about an hour alone, Chance has had enough bobbing about in the water. He climbs the wooden ladder and surveys the wharf. No Dave to be seen. He walks a sweeping arc on the wharf's rocky road, always remaining the closest person to their canoe.

A crane unloads crates from a ship. Pedestrians, mostly men, walk up and down the wharf. An occasional empty taxi cruises by blaring a reggae beat. He sees a shaded outdoor patio with diners at tables and is suddenly incredibly hungry.

Then, on the far end of the wharf, he sees Dave walking toward him. The Jamaican's head is down; he looks deep in thought.

"Hello there, mate," Chance says, feigning a pitiful Cockney accent.

"Right."

Chance drops the lame accent. "Any luck?"

"Well, we're alive, aren't we?"

"That's what I'd call minimum standard."

"You're right. Got some news. Not great. Let's get a bite."

"Think there's a place just over there."

"Any place will do."

The Broadway Café is noisy. Two women in tight pastel dresses sit at separate tables near a back wall. The gringos stand at the bar, and each orders a beer. Dave is already "a bit pissed," as he would say.

"I walked all over the wharf today trying to hitch a ride to the Island."

"I figured as much," says Chance, prodding Dave to continue.

"Talked to dockhands, baggage boys, even the dockmaster himself. No commercial vessels. Nada."

"Hmm."

"Then I found a guy in a bright blue speed boat. A beauty. Said he goes over to Corn all the time. Just not today. He was tinkering on his engine and I was watching when all of a sudden he looked up. I'm still on the dock and he says, 'Get in. Think I know someone who's going that way.'"

"Sounds promising."

"Took me on a tour of the harbor, then pulls up to a little freighter. All alone. Tied up near the back of the bay. Looks like it hasn't moved in a while."

"'Go on up,' he says. 'Yell out to the bridge. I'm sure the skipper's on board. Probably sleeping.'"

"I jump right out and head to the gangplank. Then I hear behind me 'Hey! What about me? Little something for gas?' I give him twenty córdobas and head to the boat."

Their lunch arrives at the bar. Burgers, for once. Each orders another beer.

"So. What happened?"

"After fifteen minutes, I figure out there's no one on board. My ride is gone. And I've been burned."

"*Sheeet.*"

"It was a long walk back."

The high noon crowd of noisy workers fills the restaurant. While paying their tab, Dave asks the bartender if he knows anyone going out to "the Corns." The man behind the bar says there's someone going that way almost every day. He will ask around. He tells Dave to stop by later, and Dave answers, "*Claro.*"

They spend the rest of the day tending to *Los Pumas*. Chance works on the crack in the boat's bow. He fills it with putty and creates a new patch from an empty metal can he finds in some trash. Dave scrapes away silt and muck from the waterline outside the boat.

They examine and repack personal gear. After about an hour, there is nothing more to do. They spin around the El Bluff harbor twice. Each takes a walk up and down the wharf, getting to know the area. They find a better mooring location, a spot next to an open-air boat shed where they can watch the craft from several locations on the wharf.

As afternoon shadows stretch across the sandy road, they return to the Broadway Café. The vibe inside is much more lively this time. They park themselves at a small table near the front from which they can keep an eye on the dugout. Several beer sippers listen in as a balding, silver-haired American holds court. He is dressed in coastal, casual chic: unbuttoned tropical shirt, oil-stained shorts, and open-toed sandals. He strokes a fuzzy belly between stories. Occasional laughter rips through the group.

Dave steps up to get a beer. The bartender drying mugs with a soiled towel leans in to take his order.

"*Dos Victoria, por favor.*"

"Got you covered, mate," says the barkeep.

"Glasses?"

"Naw. Bottles are fine. Keep your glasses."

"Right up, mate."

Dave lays a loose stack of cords on the bar and turns to survey the café's clientele. Across the noisy room, a barefoot man wearing a straw hat pushes coins into a jukebox. His order lands behind him with a thump. As Dave turns to grab the frosting bottles, another silver-haired gringo catches his eye.

"Quality stuff, that."

"It goes down alright," Dave grins, saluting him with a Victoria.

"Yep. Early yet."

They strike up a conversation.

Richard Harding is an American who once called Florida his home. Now he owns four boats here on the Nicaraguan coast and operates a commercial fishing business. He'd be out on the chop right now if his crew wasn't missing.

Dave explains they are heading out to Corn Island to get into the lobster trade. Right now, they are looking to hitch a ride that way.

"You're spot on," says Harding. "The Corns are the best—once you break in. Right now *El Presidente*'s son has a chokehold on the seafood traffic. But there's always room for a little competition, particularly from a 'pro' like yourself. How long have you been at it?"

Dave describes his previous trip to Corn Island. He talks about the ease with which divers go down in the clear water with no tanks and how they stay for minutes beneath the surface, coming back with lobster in each hand. He describes a water world fully stocked with "langostino," each getting plumper by the day.

Harding listens thoughtfully, splashing back shots.

"I've dug in pretty deep on the numbers. Costs for catching seafood here are nothing like back in the States. And you can hire divers for not much more than the price of these beers."

"They come. They go."

"The way I see it, I can recover my costs—except for the boat —in about half a year. Start a new life. Next year I've got a boat, maybe two. After that I'm putting money in the bank."

"Sounds like you've got a plan. After your dinner… let's talk. I could use a little help," Harding adds.

Dave grabs his change, leaves a tip, and heads back to the table with the beers. He briefs Chance on the exchange at the bar. Both agree it sounds positive, particularly given their current lack of progress.

They dine on beefsteak with rice and beans. Each dinner costs less than a buck. It is very satisfying on near-empty stomachs. Leaning back in his chair, Dave waves his new friend over.

Harding arrives at their table with a foaming pitcher. They talk about fishing, diving, and making money until the pitcher is gone. The bartender brings another.

Then their new gringo friend talks about his past.

"…been fishing for forty-something years. Started on the West Coast, Oregon. You name it, we caught it. Mackerel, salmon, even shrimp. Then up to Alaska. That was cold! Long trips. Most took three, four, five days. I was only eighteen. Back then, I could sleep anywhere. Lots of money for a guy my age. Didn't need school. Too busy. Setting traps. Dropping nets. Bringing in the big boys. But then…"

The two hopeful anglers are transported back to their own more recent pasts. Chance drifts back to classroom days and *Rime of the Ancient Mariner*. Dave feels he's once more under the spell of Lloyd Bridges in the TV show *Sea Hunt*. Harding describes vistas of open water and mortal combat that inspire the landlubbers to lean forward metaphorically into the wine-dark sea, even if it is aquamarine blue here.

"…but then, Uncle Sam had his say.

"There used to be something called 'the draft.' And it nearly got me. During those last days of the Vietnam madness, every U.S. schoolboy had to register for it. You signed up with 'the Board' and they sent you a number according to your birthday. It was a lottery with no winners."

Both Chance and Dave knew about the U.S. military draft and its dangerous numbers. Back in the day, Chance had been a prime target but got lucky and missed out on forced military service as the system ended at just the right time. Dave was immune, being Jamaican.

"When you win this draft lottery, you lose," Harding goes on.

"They drew birth dates out of a lottery drum. Made a big deal of it on TV. The lower your number, the sooner you got drafted into the military. It was a very bad deal. It all happened when you were eighteen. For a lot of guys, it meant going straight to war in Vietnam. Lots and lots never came back."

Harding drew a low number, 48. Draft numbers at the time less than 100 meant automatic enlistment unless you did something about it.

"Some guys had pull through their families. Mommy and Daddy got them out. Some guys got 'deferments' because they were sick or insane, or maybe just faked it. But for most of us, if your number got pulled, and it was less than 100, that meant you were on your way to 'Nam where all the killing was.

"And the younger you were, and if you were 'lucky' enough to be a junior officer, you'd probably wake up dead in some rice paddy there.

"My number came up I was dead meat."

Harding takes a long swill, then slams his glass down. He

tells how he made a difficult choice when his number comes up. He enlisted in the Navy.

He had lots of nautical experience and knew that Navy ships didn't cruise through rice paddies. He also knew about radios. He spent three years in service, on land, in Europe, monitoring radio signals and setting up communications sheds. He even managed to get a high-level security clearance.

"I did pretty well in the Navy. Saw lots of stuff in three years but spent most of my time wearing headphones, listening to chatter, ours and theirs. When my first tour was done, they asked me to stay. If I served another seventeen years, they said, I could retire at thirty-eight and never need to work again. But I left the Navy as fast as I could. Never looked back."

"So that's when you came here? That's when you came to Nicaragua?" Chance asks.

"Not quite."

Harding strokes the drippy sides of their third pitcher as it arrives and refills Chance's glass, then Dave's. He then takes a huge gulp from the pitcher, claiming the remainder as his own.

He went back to his family in Oregon. Eugene, near the coast. But he became restless—couldn't sit still. He found menial work with a trans-Pacific shipper. But a boat of his own was what he really wanted. He got one and went back to fishing, for himself this time, along the Pacific Coast.

"Did you know there is a Mexican California? I didn't until I went there. But first I went up and down the South American coast. To Patagonia. Around the Horn and back, with a small crew.

"But I had enough of rough seas and cold weather. Found my home here, in the Caribbean, where life is warm and easy. As long as you have a crew…

"I've got one. Actually, a crew of four. Just don't know where some of them are right now. Come on. If you want, you can help me find them. If we don't, maybe you're my new crew. You swim, don't you? Not that it's a big deal if you don't."

When the time comes to settle the tab, there is no charge for the pitchers.

"Harding took care of that, Mon," says the barman. Dave leaves a bigger tip than usual.

"I'll get the next one," says Chance.

Harding is waiting for them out on the street. It's now well past sunset. When Dave and Chance arrive, he turns, leads them to a nearby corner, and turns again, into the dark.

"What's next?"

"The place every man needs to know."

Two blocks down the dim corridor, light spills out on the sandy street, lighting a path to a restaurant called What's Yours? They catch glimpses of an open courtyard enclosed behind an eight-foot stucco wall. Palm fronds spill over the top. Vertical iron bars punctuate arched openings in the limestone wall, providing a view of activity inside.

Couples stand in shadows and sit on straw settees. Candlelit tables are tucked beneath trees. A guitar player sits on a stool, head down, eyes closed, strumming a bossa nova tune while a drummer drags brushes across a single snare. The three enter the courtyard.

"Captain Harding. Welcome," says a trim young man in an evening jacket.

"What's cooking tonight?"

"As always, whatever you want. How many are with you? Will you sit in front? Or at 'your' table?"

"Not staying. Just going inside. These are my new friends. Showing them around."

"Well, sir. You know the way."

"Sure do."

Dave marches behind Harding, who gives one table a wave. Chance follows the others, soaking in the surprising, elegant atmosphere. They arrive at the front door of an impressive home. The front steps appear to be marble, while curved cast-iron handrails direct visitors to a paneled mahogany door.

As they reach the top step, a delicate young woman in an evening gown opens the door. There are pearls at her throat. She welcomes the three rough-hewn sailors into a quiet vestibule.

"Good evening, Captain," she says, lowering her gaze.

"Evening, Missy."

"Will you be staying for the night?" Her pronunciation is impeccable but with a mild Creole lilt.

"Unfortunately, not this time. Looking for two men. You may know them…"

"The young men you are seeking I believe are already inside. They have been here for a while."

"Well, thanks. That's good news and bad. Think I'll take a look."

She leads the men down a quiet hall. Thick carpet muffles their strides. Chance hears the gentle friction of her dress as she moves, while a deep, dull noise rumbles in the distance. She stops before a wide bookcase that rises to the ceiling. She raises one manicured hand to her necklace.

"Is there anything else I can do for you? Any of you?" She asks, looking directly into the eyes of each and lingering on Chance's.

"Not just now, Missy. How about letting us in?"

She turns to face the wall filled with leather-bound books. There is an elaborate iron latch in the center of the bookcase. She slips the latch open, then pulls forward one half of the case, which is hinged to the wall, revealing a solid wooden door. She opens the door, and immediately they are absorbed in sound. People are shouting. Echoes of a rhythmic Jamaican voice bounce off every wall. It is an incredibly noisy, dimly lit bar.

Harding steps in. He signals Dave and Chance to follow.

"There they are," shouts Harding, pointing to a table beside the jukebox.

There is a full-length bar on one wall. Floor-to-ceiling curtains hang on the wall opposite the bar. Most curtains are closed. One set of drapes is drawn back to reveal a softly lit space padded with cushions.

Dancers cling together on the crowded floor. Women in colorful outfits move from table to table. One in heels, dark stockings, and tiny short shorts waves at Captain Harding. She is topless and shimmies as she waves.

Dave is spellbound. Chance is stunned. The men in the crowd are dressed casually. Some have blazers or sport jackets, but most are in relaxed attire. The women at the tables, dancing or making rounds, are dressed more colorfully. There is one glittery, blond princess with a wand. Another, this one with a feather in her hair, is dressed like Tiger Lily from *Peter Pan*.

There are salsa dancers with turbans and wraparound skirts. One walks the floor in a double-breasted business suit, smoking a cigar. None appear to be wearing blouses or shirts. A waitress taking orders at tables and a cigarette girl making rounds with a tray hanging from her neck are both naked.

Harding heads toward the jukebox. He has a large frame, so those standing in the room clear a path. Two young men are sitting alone at the table where he stops. They are the crew Harding is looking for.

The one called "Whiskey" is leaning back against the wall with only the rear legs of his chair on the ground, his face buried in a much-folded, dog-eared newspaper. "Crabmeat" is sitting, head resting neatly on folded arms, sound asleep.

Whiskey looks up when Harding blocks the dim light falling

on his paper. He takes a long, groaning stretch, then slams the paper to the table.

"I was just fixin' to call you," he yawns. "What time is it, anyway?"

"Nice turnout tonight. Pretty quiet at the dock."

"Hmm. Filled up in here since I last looked."

"It's mostly midnight."

"Wake up, Crabby Man," says Whiskey, slapping one of his companion's arms off the table.

Crabmeat's cheek hits the table surface, but he remains asleep.

"Bossman is here. Guess it's time to go to work."

"Whiskey's" given name is Winston. He was assigned the nickname not because he drinks it, but because it's easy to remember. His sober lifestyle makes him a true anomaly in this seafaring world.

Whiskey's home port is Gulf Shores, Alabama. He's been crewing as a roustabout in the Caribbean for three years. He is always in the same outfit, torn T-shirt, rolled-up khakis, bare feet. Somehow, he never needs a haircut. His dark, wavy hair always stops at the collar of his tee.

Crabmeat's real name is Crabtree. According to Whiskey, he is from Massachusetts. He wears comic round glasses that match his wry smile, even when he's asleep. His teeth have all been replaced due to a major run-in with a forklift. His alcohol consumption makes up for the abstinence of his partner. He is a favorite with bartenders, at least when he remembers to tip. Whiskey and Crabmeat generally ship out and take time out together, except on rare occasions when one or the other disappears with a woman. Except for those rare occasions, Whiskey and Crabmeat are inseparable.

"No need to wake Crabmeat. I got me a new crew. Meet Dave and... uh..."

"Chance."

"Yeah... meet Chance here"

"Right." Whiskey says to Harding, then, "C'mon, Crabby!! Time to go."

"No. I'm serious. Meet the new crew... Dave and, uh, the other one."

Whiskey finally rouses Crabmeat enough to have him stand.

Crabby bats his eyes twice behind his round glasses, grins at Harding, the new acquaintances, and the rest of the room, then collapses back in his chair. Whiskey raises his partner and, executing a perfect fireman's lift, hoists him to his shoulder.

They all leave the deafening room.

An hour later, Dave and Chance hang their hammocks at Harding's covered boat slip at the end of the commercial dock. They understand they have been used as foils to get Harding's boat hands back to work.

But the travelers have been adequately compensated with food and beer throughout the evening. Having a place to hang their hammocks out of the weather until morning is an added bonus. Harding has also gotten in touch with one of his colleagues, whose commercial freighter *Nicky C.* is scheduled to depart for Corn Island the next day around 9 a.m.

Chance drifts off to sleep with an evening breeze swaying his hammock, thinking about names: Whiskey, Crabmeat, and his own.

CHOPPY SEAS

C hance cannot ignore the clattering and rumbling on the dock, even though it's barely dawn. He digs out his flashlight, shines it around, and struggles to remember where he is. His head is throbbing. His throat feels like sandpaper. Dave is nowhere to be seen. His hammock is empty, his rucksack gone.

Chance peels off his hammock and checks his pockets. Pastel clouds wash pale color across the sky. He is hungry.

Leaving the covered boat slip, Chance moves through foot traffic to the Broadway Café. A smiling woman welcomes him from the kitchen and points to Dave seated alone on the open-air porch. He orders: "Coffee, very black." She fills a cup and slides it to him across the counter.

"Gracias."

"De nada. It is best in all Caribbean. Grown upriver, near Rama. You call me Missus."

It is maybe 8 a.m., but Chance's shirt is already clinging to his back and under his arms.

"Your friend? He waits for you."

She points again to Dave, who is hovering over his table, engrossed in paperwork. They are the only diners in the Café.

"You are the ones looking for pull to Corn Island, I think. There is a ship sailing to Corn today. Leaving soon. You will have breakfast? *Huevos? Pescado fresco?*"

"Just eggs, beans, and rice. Thanks. I'll come get it when you're ready."

"You sit. I bring."

He doesn't question how this woman he's never met is aware of the details of their trip. It seems everyone at every turn knows their business. He wonders if his creased brow makes his thoughts transparent. Chance joins Dave.

"So, Sleeping Beauty, how was the nap?"

"Almost enough... What happened last night? Did I dream it all?"

"Old news. Listen, I was just coming to get you. We need to find a lift. Ships... big ones, small freighters, all sizes go to Corn Island every day. We're losing time."

Chance looks out from the shade at the passing parade. All colors seem faded by bright sunlight. Soon Missus appears at the table with a large platter of food, everything Chance ordered plus more.

"I bring you fish. Is same price. You need food."

She walks away, leaving Chance wondering when people will finally listen to what he says and take him at his word. He wonders when people, even strangers, will stop assuming that they know better about him than he does.

Corn Island is seventy kilometers due east across the Caribbean from El Bluff. The waters near the mainland are choked with sandbars and coral reefs. Abundant sea life cruises the shallow waters, frothy with sea foam, turning from pale aqua at the surface to rich sapphire below.

There are snapper, grouper, and jacks, colorful sergeant majors, parrotfish, yellowtail and bluejack, and odd-looking trunkfish and triggerfish. Apart from that, spotted eagle rays and stingrays patrol the bottom, looking like misplaced matadors.

With any aquatic community, there are also predators. Giant green moray eels lurk in coral caves. Great barracuda cruise singly or in packs, grinning with sinister underbites at potential meals. The gentle blue waters are also free range for all kinds of shark. The nurse is docile and harmless. Caribbean reef sharks can be seen everywhere. There are lemon, bull, and clumsy-looking hammerheads. Tiger sharks enjoy wintering along the Caribbean coast because of the temperate climate. In January, tigers are particularly plentiful.

Dave is not concerned about the dangers in the water. He is intent on establishing a financial beachhead on Corn Island and developing a personal dynasty there. Chance, on the other hand, has always seen this trip as a unique, unlikely adventure with nothing personal at stake. The two are not at cross purposes, simply in parallel pursuit of their future selves.

Although they learn locals make the trip back and forth between Bluffton and Corn Island daily in open speedboats and even paddle craft, the journey is far too risky for inexperienced sailors.

So Dave is exuberant when he comes running back to the shed later that morning.

"Got us another tow! Get your shit together. Leaving in about three hours. Can't miss this one. Called the *Max 5*. It's a 'tramper' and leaving sooner than *Nicky C.* Taking diesel over to Corn. C'mon. Let's go."

"How appropriate for this place, and us... a tramper," Chance says.

Dave climbs into the dugout, takes his seat at the rear, and gives the motor a lucky pat. He inspects the fuel tank and its spare, primes the pump, and cranks the engine with one pull. Chance releases lines and climbs in. It takes only minutes to shove off.

At the helm, Dave executes a graceful but rapid turn in the still water. There is lots of activity at the marina now. Fishers thump barefoot with bait, food for the day, and coolers with ice. The wake from *Los Pumas* makes other small boats bob in the water. Shrimpers tend nets. Workers on other boats slosh water on decks with large buckets.

There's one much larger vessel riding low in the water at the end of the pier with its bow pointing east. Chance does not remember seeing it on the day they arrived, nor the day before during their walks up and down the dock.

Steam spills from the top of the coastal tanker *Max 5* and drifts inland over Bluefield's bay. The ship is the length of two football fields laid end to end, and, while small compared to other tankers and freighters at sea, it dwarfs everything else here at El Bluff. A smokestack sits above the bridge from which the captain guides the vessel. A crew of three uses a steel crane near the bow to lift containers from dock to deck.

The surfaces above the deck are rusty white, while the parts below are black and peeling. A communication tower bristling with antennae sits at the boat's rear. Another tower with a ladder and observation platform rises at the front of the ship, while massive chains fore and aft secure *Max 5* to the pier.

Dave pulls their noble dugout *Los Pumas* along *Max 5*'s rusty side, and Chance grabs the bottom tread of a suspended ladder near the waterline where there is a strong current and an unnerving amount of chop. Dave kills the motor, clambers forward on all fours, and quickly mounts the ladder. Once on deck, he looks down to the rocking dugout—which has never looked so small—and shouts out to Chance over crashing waves and mounting engine noise.

"Just hold here. Tight. Got to find the captain again. Need to load our gear on board."

"OK. What about the boat?"

"I'll find out about that too," he yells through cupped hands.

The turbulence on the water has increased dramatically since the day before. Gray flannel clouds push inland. The bay appears more confrontational than serene.

Chance loops a rope through the tanker's ladder and takes out the slack. Moving carefully, using hands as well as feet, he moves to the stern, hunkers down where Dave normally sits, and looks out to sea. He takes a moment to absorb and reflect.

He remembers how his mostly absentee father once told him, "Every day is different on the water." For years, Chance has tried to disprove the statement with no success. Today is very much different, weather-wise and water-wise, than just the day before.

"It's why you don't live life with the covers over your head," he thinks, quoting his father once again. For perhaps the hundredth time, Chance notes how much wiser his father has become since he passed away.

Dave clambers down the ladder like a motivated ape.

"OK. We got the 'green light.' We're good to go."

"Thought we already were. You said we had a tow."

"Well. We had it from the skipper. But he had to check with his boss by radio. Now we're off!"

Just then, a grinning face peers over the chain rail above. The face disappears, and a wooden skid is lowered by block and tackle to the dugout. Dave grabs the small wooden platform and rests it on the front gunwales of their dugout.

"Load everything on this skid. It's going up on the deck."

Soon all their gear is on board. Then, three ropes drop down the side of the tramper. Chance and Dave tie lines tightly around

87

Los Pumas. Checking the knots many times, they climb the ladder and stand on deck. An electric winch hauls the dugout up top to the open foredeck.

They tie *Los Pumas* tightly to containers that are stacked and chained in place. All seems ready for departure. They find a steel bench facing forward at the base of the bridge and place their rucksacks beneath it. There, they sit out of everyone's way and wait for departure. In minutes, Chance is asleep, but Dave stays stiffly alert.

Around 11 a.m., activity on the tanker deck comes to a halt. A deckhand climbs the forward metal tower. Another stakes out a post near the bow's anchor line. A third hand heads to the stern. Dave and Chance remain at their posts on the bench. Three excruciating blasts come from the ship's horn. Then three more pierce the morning air.

Now engines rumble. The tanker pulls away from the dock like a scab from a sore, riding low in the water. It maintains a wide berth around other rocking boats. Giant winches rattle as they pull up mooring chains. The tanker eases into the bay and finds a channel marked with buoys, heading steadily toward the open sea.

"This is it! We're off!"

"Sure looks that way."

The two soon find it impossible to sit still. They go to the handrail, look over the side, and see *Los Pumas* bound tightly on the low riding tanker deck. They look beyond the sound out to sea. It's too noisy to speak. Dave leans forward, hands clenched behind his back, eyes squinting, and teeth gritted; he looks like a proud figurehead surging toward destiny.

As the tanker increases speed, Chance notices a broad patch of unruly waves ahead. Soon the tanker bucks a bit as it crosses a reef. The waves grow larger, bashing against the portside hull, and water washes across the deck. *Los Pumas* also begins to twitch. The waves grow stronger and higher, smashing against the dugout's hull. Chance hears ropes squeak as they strain against mighty pressure from the surf.

One large wave completely covers the dugout. Then another and another batter their vulnerable canoe. An enormous wave crashes against the side. This one sends spray across the tanker deck and into Dave and Chance's disbelieving eyes. Yet another, even larger, wave targets the little dugout, smashing it viciously. The young men move forward but can only watch.

One restraining line around *Los Pumas* now comes undone. They hear planking snap. The recently repaired crack in the dugout's bow widens. Another restraining line comes undone. The little boat is suddenly wrenched around backward. Two more large waves wash onboard, flooding the entire tanker deck with water. The dugout slips out of its last restraining line and floats free as the tanker gains speed moving forward.

The captain opens a window on the bridge, leans out, and shouts, "I can't go back, now, Mon." He then slams the window shut.

They race along the rail to the rear of the deck. *Los Pumas* is bobbing freely in the tramper's wake, unrestrained. There is nothing the adventurers can say or do but stand at the stern and watch the dugout float away.

A thousand córdobas, lost at sea.

Chance feels keen empathy for Dave, who remains very still as he leans again over the rail, striking the same figurehead pose as moments earlier, but now with a very different vision of the future.

WASHED
ASHORE

It takes nearly five hours for *Max 5* to arrive at the commercial dock of *Isla de Maiz Grande*, the larger of the two islands known as "Big Corn" and "Little Corn" to residents. The closest landmasses apart from the Nicaraguan mainland are Cuba to the north, Jamaica to the northeast, Colombia, Panama, and Costa Rica to the south.

"The Corns" have provided refuge for pirates, plunderers, and nonconformists like Dave and Chance for centuries. The islands were "protected" by the British Crown from the mid-1600s until 1860. They are just off the Mosquito Coast, and annoying insects *are* a problem, although the name actually derives from the Moskito indigenous people of the region.

When the United States entered the war in 1914, the islands and nearby coasts were leased to the country for ninety-nine years, mostly as a strategic precaution. However, the U.S. engagement during that period was minimal. When strongman president Anastasio Somoza Debayle denounced the Bryan–Chamorro Treaty on Bastille Day, 1970, no one particularly cared. The U.S., its Central American neighbors, and the world collectively shrugged their shoulders.

At that time, international attention was firmly directed toward Southeast Asia and was only mildly diverted by student uprisings in European capitals and U.S. college campuses. Back then, Chance had never paid any attention to Nicaragua or heard of the Corn Islands, and Dave only knew of them as some islands near his home in Kingston.

The islands are small and idyllic but not easy to access. The larger of the two is only about four square miles and can easily be circumnavigated by foot in a day, with the biggest obstacles being the beach bars.

Mount Pleasant Hill, on the north of Big Corn, is the highest point, almost four hundred feet in elevation. Lookout Point on Little Corn Island, at about 125 feet, is the best spot to stand and wave at family and friends on Big Corn. The population on the Corns is only a couple of thousand, all descendants of pirates, Caribbean Creoles, and indigenous sorts.

Big Corn has an airport, but rustic Little Corn does not. The only way to get there is by boat, and the only way to get around is on foot. There are no vehicles.

Afternoons are a good time to take naps because of the regular tropical showers. Predictably, most independent commercial enterprises are in U.S. citizens' hands or are Chinese-owned. The family of *El Presidente*, General Anastasio Somoza, owns the largest money-maker, a fish processing enterprise called Promarblu. It is considered a vital, strategic national asset.

As the afternoon sun disappears behind monumental clouds, *Max 5* moves quickly through the Caribbean chop. Sea foam flows behind the big boat like giant mermaid locks, leaving a clean, triangular wake to the west. Two tiny landmasses appear directly ahead of the ship's bow.

Dave and Chance sit on the metal bench they have occupied

all day. They are quiet for most of the trip. There is little to be said about their recent disaster at sea.

"Damn, I feel bad," Chance says as they approach Big Corn.

"What about? Beans in your belly?"

"Well, that too."

"Not as bad as I do."

Dave squints at the sea, the sky, and the island ahead. Chance feels like he did something wrong and needs to be punished. He wants a mature voice to speak up and put this disaster behind them.

"I should have known. I should have had more lines on the dugout. Tied everything tighter. Should have tied it behind rather than on the side of the boat."

"The captain told you where to strap it. I tied some of those damn ropes too. Don't beat yourself. Does no good. We'll get another."

"But still... will there be other canoes on Corn? You've put everything into this. I'm just along for the ride."

"There are lots of boats. Everyone has a boat. Some families have several, in different sizes. That's not the problem. The real problem is money. We need to get to work sooner now. Build traps. Get 'em in the water. Catch those langosta. Build bonds with the fishmongers."

Engines pulse below deck and rhythmic surf is parted by *Max 5*'s prow. The day is still warm, but a fresh breeze in their faces keeps the travelers cool. A party of dolphins escorts them eastward. Bristly palm trees appear above the landmass ahead, and a brilliant white sand beach separates jungle from the sea.

Within the hour, they are standing on the dock. Dave has spoken with the captain to make sure *Max 5* will be here until morning for unloading of diesel and container goods. Then the ship will depart for ports farther south. He confirms their gear is fine in the forward compartment for now, but they should come early in the morning to retrieve it before off-loading begins in earnest.

"Let's get something to eat. Suddenly I'm starved."

"OK. But first we need to find Nelly's guest house. Hope she's got room. If not, I know some other spots but Nelly is nice. Stayed there last time."

They walk along the dock of Puerto de Corn Island. The convergence of multiple cultures is evident in the name. Three other large vessels are moored with ramps to the harbor. There are stacks of freight on the skids and the dock. Deckhands on one ship stand by as goods from its hold are lowered to land by a crane.

A long-limbed man peddles by on a tricycle; a sign with the hand-painted word "TAXI" hangs from the rear. He makes eye contact with Chance and rings a bell. Chance waves him away but thinks that one day soon this will be a great way to tour the island.

Promarblu Fish Processing Factory is at the hub of the pier. Dave and Chance peer in the glass front of a door marked "Cafeteria." It is closed but due to reopen at 4:30 a.m. They move along the street and find a general store and many bars. A street sign points the way to *Vía Principal*. Another sign points to "Dock for Little Corn Island."

The word *"Presidente"* is everywhere. There are posters in windows reading *"!Viva!"* and "Presidente Forever!" Portraits of a man in military garb dripping with medals adorn T-shirts in restaurants and ice chests in stores. A recent unopposed election has just assured another seven-year tenure for the strong-arm president. On the surface, at least, he is well loved here.

They receive polite smiles and calm waves from men sitting on benches in front of quiet warehouses with wide-open doors. The path splits, and Dave turns away from the shore. Within a few dozen strides, Chance hears children playing and sees a shady compound with wood houses.

Dave steps up on the porch of the first, peers into the screen door, and then knocks. The children are suddenly quiet; he knocks again, and a dark shadow fills the screen.

"Miss Nelly here?"

"Just a moment." The large form turns and disappears.

It takes a moment, but soon, the screen is filled again, this time with a slighter figure.

"Miss Nelly?"

"Ah... Mistah..."

"Kipling... Dave Kipling... I was here before—last year. You had a place for me. Here..."

"Yes. Yes. Yes. Mistah Jamaica. Yes. Yes."

"I told you I'd be back. And here I am. Only this time, it's me and one more." He points to Chance.

The screen door screeches open. A slender woman of indeterminate age steps out on the porch. She has sharp, chiseled features. Her hair is tied back in a colorful wrap. She wears a muted floral dress, buttoned up the front, open at the throat and knee, and no shoes.

"Well... yes, you did. And yes, you are. You are back. This time to stay, I know it. And with a friend."

"We've come to fish. Fish for lobster. And... I am hoping you have a place for us. Here."

"Yes. Yes. Of course. Only... you must stay together. This is...?"

"This is Chance. My partner. He comes from the United States. He knows a lot about fishing. We are here to do business."

"Oh. I see." Nelly offers Chance her hand.

He shakes it and grins sheepishly.

"Mr. Chance... Mr. United States... Mr. USA."

They follow her around the back of her home, where there are three smaller versions. She takes them to the one farthest from the main house and closest to the jungle. She opens the

94

plank door and steps up onto the raised wooden floor. They follow. There are two rooms, one with two metal cots and a small table, the other with a table and stool. One wall in this room has open shelves.

"This one I save for you, Mistah. I know you come back… with a friend. I show you bath."

They examine a primitive outhouse. Above a raised floor, there is a wooden seat with no lid. Vertical boards enclosing the outhouse stop a foot from the roof. There is no screen to keep out bugs.

A well with short daub retaining walls stands a few strides from the outhouse. A ceramic sink with a bucket on a rope is close by. Chance drops the bucket into the dark well, hears it splash, then draws it up. The water is clear, but probably suitable only for washing.

"How much will you take for this?"

"Is twenty córdobas…"

"Ouch…"

"Is twenty… for the week… for both… a fair price?"

The wanderers confer briefly. The quoted rate is the equivalent of about $1.50. Dave continues his tough negotiation.

"Thank you, Miss Nelly. I think we will take it."

"You make me happy."

Chance hands their new landlord a twenty-córdoba note. Dave confirms the details with Miss Nelly. There is a propane gas stove they can use in the main house. They can drink water from the well, but only after boiling it. She gives him the one key to the door the two gringos will share. And there are plenty of churches all around.

"Catholic, Moravian… Jehovah's Witness is right next to the airport."

The young men drop their bags on their bunks.

"Let's get some grub. Big day tomorrow."

The smooth crooning of a reggae singer attracts them to an open-air restaurant called the Fishin' Hole. They walk inside, and a pale man behind the bar waves them over. A series of mirrors behind the bar makes the space feel more spacious than it actually is. Stuffed fish heads, giant conch shells, rods with reels, and lobster baskets crowd the walls, which also display more stern posters of *El Presidente*.

"Knew it wouldn't be long. What can I pour you?"

"Let's see what you have. Whaddya mean, wouldn't be long?"

"Oh. Saw you guys get off the big boat, then look in the Promarblu cafeteria window. They close at three. Everybody here on this end of the island goes home for dinner. Didn't see no picnic basket, so I figured you'd be looking for food."

Lyle, the owner of the Fishin' Hole, gives them a well-worn spiel. He came here two years ago from the States and has been on ships ever since he could drive a forklift. Got sick of it. Headed down through Mexico to see the Southern Hemisphere. Met a woman on "the other side of Nic." She brought him here. Then she left.

"So I opened this bar... now, what'll ya have?"

Chance is struck once again by how everyone seems to know their business better than he does. He orders a hamburger, fried plantain, and a strawberry rosita. Dave asks for another beer, having already drained his first.

The island's newest residents, Dave and Chance, eventually head back to Nelly's, following the bouncing beam of a pocket "torch." The jungle is now dark and slightly menacing. There are sounds of animals moving through the leaves. Night birds call and coo. Chance collapses on his cot and is asleep before the sky goes completely dark. Dave makes a few notes on his pocket pad before dousing his light.

Transporting their stowed property to Nelly's takes all the next day, much of the time spent thanking, resisting, and finally fighting off offers of assistance from locals. Dave is offered the use of a car, but he declines because the cost of gas here is "so dear."

It's clear Dave is feeling the pinch of having to purchase or rent another boat. Chance offers some help, but his resources are more limited than Dave's. And, after all, Chance is only the "tagalong." Dave is the one who intends to make a fortune here. Chance is now planning to attend graduate school in film when he returns from the Caribbean.

They pick up what they can, but large, heavy items are left for another trip. Chance estimates that the journey on foot across the harbor and through the jungle is approximately a mile and a half. Dave assures him it is much more. They are wringing wet with sweat when they return to their new quarters in the jungle. Nelly's children watch from the porch with wide, shy eyes.

They return to the tanker. Entering the forward chamber once again, they survey the fishing gear, Styrofoam floats, camping essentials, tarps, tools, spare fuel tank, and clothes that are scattered about. It has clearly been "inspected" by someone else. They gather all that remains.

Now, back outside, Chance pays the cost of a "jitney," one of the oversized tricycles that cruise up and down the dock. It takes the two vagabonds and their remaining stuff to Nelly's. At the cost of one U.S. dollar, the ride is a bargain. They separate their things (most of which belong to Dave), shove as much as possible under the cots, then make a pile in the kitchen room.

"Thank God that's done. I'm starved. Let's go eat."

"Think I'll stay here. Feeling a little queasy," says Chance.

"Alright. Just don't drink any water."

The truth is that Chance feels fine. He just needs a little space. He has discovered that he and Dave run on different clocks and different agendas. He's eaten enough for the day.

A bit later, standing beside Nelly's well at the outdoor basin, Chance finds a cracked, wood-stained remnant of soap. He washes his chest, arms, and neck and faces the rising moon. He rinses and feels surprisingly refreshed in the mild Caribbean breeze.

TWO CASTAWAYS FIND A HOME

O n his back, nearly awake, Chance floats through a flood of sensation. Chirping birds harmonize with the voices of children, floral essences twine together in fragrances he has never smelled, the sea breeze bristles the fabric on his bare skin, sea salt tickles his tongue, and shadowy images dance across his closed eyes.

Tattered rags of disconnected dreams drift through his brain. Each is powerful and brightly colored. He is part of some grand enterprise, but the objective is unclear. He summons forces, his own and those of others, to drive toward some undetermined goal. There are faces of women from his past but few men, and those have no faces.

A deep voice declares, "A man must eat."

The dream fragments fade, replaced by impressions from the day before. Loading, then unloading, gear on the tramper, tying complicated knots that refuse to stay taut, disaster at sea, and Dave's sharp, wind-stroked features peering beyond the horizon. Profound disappointment. Chance groans, opens his eyes, focuses slowly on the rafters beneath a tin roof, and once again hears a cacophony of birdcalls.

Chance looks over at the other bunk and sees Dave, who, for once, is sound asleep. It's a Thursday, mid-January, the twenty-fifth day of their journey. He fishes for essentials beneath his bed. They're all there; the leather pouch with passport, checks, and cash is beneath his pillow. He finds his day book and makes a few notes that end with the words "Finally on Corn Island."

He steps quietly across the wooden floor, opens the door, and bolts quickly for the outhouse. Outside, the air is almost cool but still thick. The shadows from the jungle are dark. The atmosphere is lush but alien.

The door on the wooden "loo" stands ajar. He steps inside as his innards rumble with anticipated relief. There is a damp, organic odor, which he does not find offensive. He crouches above the moldy oval, not wanting to touch it. There is near-instant satisfaction. It has been four days since evacuation of this sort. He hears movement in the small cavern below but does not look down.

Outside, Chance draws clear water from the well. He splashes his face but resists the temptation to sip the water. He turns toward the sun and basks in an easterly breeze. The sound of surf calls out to him through palm and banana trees.

After a short walk, he stands on a sparkling white beach looking out across the Caribbean. The sun has completely cleared the sharp horizon. Soft sudsy waves break at the shore. Others, rising above a reef, illuminated from behind, are lime green. They race to the shore.

The beach is littered with palm fronds and coconuts. Chance leaves his sneakers behind, walks to the surf, splashes seawater on his face, turns, kicks at the water, and jogs up to a bend a quarter mile away. He sees other neatly tended houses like Nelly's, most with yards facing the sea. He turns and jogs back, feeling the sun on his arms, neck, and face. Chance makes a mental note—"Day One on Corn Island"—and goes back to find his shoes.

Back at the hut now called home, Dave is ready to rip.

"Morning, mate. Hope you're ready for a big one."

"Let's do it."

"Breakfast first. Then retrieve our gear. If it's still there, I put some things on your bunk to look over. Lots to do, so gotta get on with it. All set?"

There are now drawings on Chance's cot. He's seen them before, precise sketches of fish traps with minute handwritten dimensions. For a moment, he sits and studies them. For the first time, they seem to make sense. Before now, they were only an abstraction.

Dave confidently leads the way back to the pier, where the workday is well underway. Containers are being loaded. A forklift squeals as it goes back and forth on the dock. Workers laugh and shout; they appear happy to work.

Inside the Promarblu cafeteria, there's a clock on the wall showing local time to be 8:15. Dave and Chance load basic dockhand meals on plastic trays: beans, eggs, coffee, sweet bread. Dave remarks that six córdobas for breakfast is a little more expensive than he remembers.

They plan their day:

- Check gear.
- Take what they can carry and stow it at Nelly's.
- Find a boat for hire.
- Transport remaining big stuff (outboard motor, fuel tanks, fishing, and camping gear) also to temporary storage at Nelly's.

Then, if there's time, they will shop for more materials and begin to build traps. Sounds easy over a cup of coffee.

They spend the rest of the morning roaming the island, looking for a boat. They patrol the pier to no avail. Most active workers here come from other parts. There are no leads back at the cafeteria, either. The Chinese owner of the general store suggests they check out the noticeboard there. However, they find only boats for sale, none for rent or daily use. And their current pocket cash is too low for another purchase.

They head north along the shore, away from the pier. Dave knows of other clusters of homes facing out from the island's leeward side, some with vessels parked on the beach at an inlet called Brig Bay. Careful to stay beneath shady palms, they find a young man in his teens working on an overturned dugout. They stop to talk.

Henri is strapping and angular, over six feet tall, with long, muscular arms. He pauses his work to greet the strangers with a broad smile. They exchange comments about the weather, the breeze, and the sea. Dave admires the canoe's curved keel.

"Looks like a fine day to be on the water."

"It was," Henri agrees. "Still is. But the lobster now sleeps."

Henri describes his day so far. It is not yet noon, but Henri has already had a full one. He was on the water well before dawn. He and two partners dive for "langosta" as early as possible, every day except Sunday. They catch by hand as the crustaceans make their way back home to crevices in the coral. Morning is the best time for catching.

Dave points to a pile of wire mesh traps. Henri explains that they use those too but that catching "with fingers is best." Dave nods and thoughtfully agrees. This is all new to Chance.

"We are new to the island."

"Yes. I can see."

"We are looking for a boat. To fish for langosta."

"Maybe you use one of mine," Henri says, pointing to two other overturned craft on the shore.

"We would like that very much. Can we try one out?"

In minutes, Henri and Dave are on the water. Chance stays behind. The young local stands in the rear navigating with a giant wood paddle as they fight through breaking waves. Dave sits forward, looking back, watching the Corn Islander's technique. Henri offers the paddle to Dave, who crawls to the rear of the boat. With two giant strides, Henri steps forward. There is a bit of a wobble. Dave holds on tight, takes the paddle, and immediately tries to push the vessel forward. Henri watches and grins.

"You must stand."

"But I don't have the balance," the new helmsman shouts. He rises tentatively. He tries to use the long paddle but clearly finds it heavy, awkward. Waves begin to turn the dugout sideways and push it back to shore.

"Push, Mon, push. You must push. Let me show."

Dave hands his young tutor the paddle.

With a few vigorous strokes, they are again heading to sea. Henri gives the paddle back to Dave. Now, leaning against the seat, Dave crouches and manages painfully to inch the boat forward.

"Turn us around, Mon. Back to the beach. I think you have it."

By now, Chance has met Henri's father, Alexandro, his mother, and a few brothers at the shore. Dave beaches the dugout as Henri steps over the bow and pulls it forward from the chop. The group gathers. They strike a deal for rental—five córdobas for the day. Chance is amazed by the casual nature of the agreement. Dave resists his natural inclination to improve it.

"I like to help everybody. And so my mother... and father. You pay me when you bring back the canoe."

Everyone helps with the launch. Dave, now skipper of the

vessel, hands Chance a second long-handled paddle. Together, they make their way over the surf and out to smoother water. From there, they can easily see *Max 5*, which is waiting at the dock with the rest of their gear.

The tramper *Max 5* remains in the near distance for a long time. Tide, current, and a lack of navigational knowledge work against them. The two apprentice seamen spend two hours paddling before returning to the Corn Island wharf.

Dave spots a place to tie up. The tide is high, but still; they climb a narrow ladder to reach the busy deck. They dodge non-stop forklift and pull-cart traffic and wave at familiar faces as they scale *Max 5*'s gangplank. They cross her deck, slide down multiple ladders, and make their way once more to the hold. They see their gear pushed to one side in the forward compartment. Other boxes and bags are piled closer to the door.

"Outboard motor first."

It's a struggle to remove the motor from the ship. It's more than a two-person job. Passages are narrow, there are ladders to climb and descend, and fragrant bodies jam every space. Finally, they gently lay the outboard in the center of the bouncing canoe.

"I'll strap it down later. Let's go get the rest."

"Think it will be alright there?"

"Of course, these people are honest."

Wringing with sweat, they return to the hold to grab camping gear, tools, and other essentials and then head once again to the dock. Their borrowed canoe bobs alongside *Max 5*. It looks lower in the water than before. Dave stands in the boat. Chance hands down the gear.

"Tide's going out."

"How can you tell?"

"You must learn to notice these things. Look at the sun, it's well past noon."

Chance grows silent, then glum. He is tired of Dave telling him what to do.

They return to the hold and gather more gear. They repeat the canoe loading sequence. As Dave stands in the boat, Chance hands down bags. They say nothing and return to the hold a final time. Dave makes a long, critical inspection.

"Gah-dammit. Stuff's missing."

"It's all in the canoe."

"No, it's not. The can filled with gas. The bag with my blades. They're gone! Gah-dammit! Damn Teefs!"

Dave is right. There was a spare tank filled with gasoline. It's gone. In addition, Dave's "special" leather pouch, which held the machete with a hand-carved handle he bought in La Union, is missing. They have not loaded those items onto the canoe.

"Let's ask the captain."

"Won't do any damn good. Damn Teefs. Let's get out of here. Now!"

For once, Chance is inclined to agree. The captain won't know. Returning to the canoe, they confirm the gas tank and leather pouch are not there. Dave seethes with anger.

Chance covers their possessions with a tarp and tightens the rope around it, all without speaking a word. He grabs the bowline, unties it, leaves it looped around the dock cleat, and takes his seat forward. A paddle lies by his feet.

Dave pushes off from the stern. His "mate" lets the bowline go slack, then pulls it on board. They paddle hard toward the open Caribbean.

The wind has picked up. Their course takes them into breaking waves. With each surge of surf, spray wets the boat. Water collects around their feet.

"Bail, Chance. Bail. Gah-dammit... to hell!"

Chance puts down his paddle and bails with a coffee can. He

finds another and bails water over the side of the boat with two hands.

Dave paddles like a man possessed. He guides the canoe away from the harbor, then turns it north, back toward the inlet where they began. Chance bails water furiously but can't keep up. Water now covers his shins. Dave puts down his paddle, grabs a can from Chance, scoops water, and pours it over the side. He scoops and pours much more quickly than his partner.

"Faster, man. Faster."

With no paddling from the stern, the boat quickly goes broadside to the waves: one, two, three lap over the side. The dugout rocks dangerously with each wave. Dave jumps quickly to the rear. With an effort, he turns the boat to again point directly into the wind and waves. The water in the bottom is now up to their shins.

"Keep bailing, man. Faster. I have to stay back here and paddle."

The boat slowly makes headway back toward Brig Bay. Chance bails but cannot keep up with the flooding as wave after wave laps over the rail. The boat now lies low in the water. Chance begins to think that they really could sink and bails as fast as he can, as if his life depends on this effort. He looks back at Dave, who squints and remains amazingly calm. Soon Brig Bay is in sight.

Chance sees tall, slender Henri standing in the surf, as sturdy as a sunburnt statue watching the sailors' approach. There are two tall, lean men behind him. They roll palm tree trunks into the surf and create a sequence of them on the beach, heading toward the jungle.

"It's Henri."

"I know. I'm not surprised. He's worried about his boat."

Wind whips Chance's hair around his head. Dave paddles harder now that he's seen Henri and the team onshore. Henri waves at the boat with its rookie crew. He points toward the tree trunks lying in parallel formation out of the surf, onto the beach, and beyond the high-water line. Now Henri stands in water to his waist. Wind from the north has picked up dramatically.

"Forget bailing. Grab your paddle. Stroke like hell."

"We're filling up. We're going down."

"Shut up and stroke. We're not going down."

"We're flooded. We're going to sink!!"

"Paddle!"

"We're sinking."

"Shut up! We're not sinking. The boat is made of wood. Wood floats. We're not going to sink."

The canoe is completely flooded but remains afloat. Gear bobs near the surface, held in place only by sisal lines. Wind and surf drown out encouraging voices from the shore. A crowd of faces collects along the jungle's edge.

Henri and helpers pantomime various actions. One mimics throwing an imaginary rope. Henri points emphatically toward the palm trunk logs. Two others sweep their arms along the path of the logs. Dave directs the canoe toward the improvised ramp as they enter shallow water.

Henri swims to the boat's prow and hangs on. He begins to swim the boat back to shore. Dave and Chance paddle with all their might. Only the boat's gunwales are now visible with the floating tarp—and they disappear with each wave.

The anxious paddlers continue making headway to shore. In moments, Henri gains a foothold in the sand. Soon he is standing, then walking as Chance and Dave continue to paddle. Finally, a strong wave raises the dugout, thrusts it forward, and rams it into the sand. They are beached.

Two of Henri's brothers approach the boat with more logs. They drop them in the water near the bow. Now Henri's helpers push the dugout onto the submerged tree trunks. Another brother arrives toting two five-gallon paint buckets. With the efficiency that comes with experience, two more helpers empty water from the canoe in minutes.

"Hop out onto the sand, Mon," says Henri. "Looks like you had quite a ride."

Holding their paddles, Dave and Chance do as suggested and collapse on the sand. Chance marvels that somehow, they have dodged another monstrous bullet. Dave studies the sand where he sits.

Grinning broadly, Henri stands before them. His companions draw the boat further up the beach by rolling it over the parade of tree trunks. Another young man waits just past the high-water mark, beside a handmade wooden cart with large rubber tires. When the boat, still loaded with gear, reaches the cart, all look back toward Henri and wait.

"The afternoon wind, she is strong from the east," says Henri. "At this time of year, morning is best for the sail."

"So I see," says Dave.

"You have learned much about Corn today."

"That is certain."

"But we are here to help. You can stay for dinner. And I have a place for you to keep your equipment. These are my brothers." He points at a line of young men standing in the sand, waiting for direction.

"They will make your equipment safe, but first it must dry."

TRAPPER JACK

"Trapper Jack, the Jamaican" broods over his work as though it were an adversary. He is a large man whose heavy brow casts a constant shadow over his broad nose. Short sleeves display powerful biceps. He tucks nails to be used for weaving his fish traps into a kinked forelock. He neither smiles nor laughs as he works.

Dave and Chance sit spellbound in front of Jack's office, a simple frame shed with three wooden sides beneath a tight circle of palms. They are all sitting in the sand. With no hesitation and no second thoughts, Jack builds a trap specifically designed to catch Caribbean lobster (here called "langosta" or "langoustine") from materials provided by Dave. It is a simple, time-proven contraption allowing one way in and no way out for curious sea creatures. The trap is completed in minutes from hardware mesh, baling wire, and nylon cord. Nails are used as needles to stitch the structure together.

"Amazing, Jack. Will you make another?"

Jack grunts as Dave hands the burly fisherman more wire. He

sets to the task without looking up, legs outstretched in the sun-bleached sand, powerful knees bracing the assembly before him like a giant vise.

They had met Jack the previous night at the Fishin' Hole, having been introduced by owner Lyle, who called him "the best trap builder and lobster catcher on the island." Lyle, another transplanted gringo, has grown friendly with the recent U.S. arrivals during their daily refreshment stop.

"You also have something important in common," Lyle had said.

"Really? What might that be?"

"Jamaica."

Dave had stepped up to a booth where Jack was holding court. Here, a bunch of young men were chatting loudly, talking on top of each other. They were spinning bottles on the floor and piling shrimp shells on the table. Jack occupied the entire back bench of the booth facing the room. He watched as Dave approached with two beers in each hand.

"*Wah gwan?*" Dave asked in casual island street talk.

The table quickly fell quiet. Lyle watched from the bar.

"As you see," Jack said, sweeping his long arms across the table. Then he asked, "Will you join us, Mon?"

"Delighted," said Dave.

Two more chairs appeared at the table. Dave and Chance spent the rest of the evening speaking with Jack and company about fish traps, ganja in Jamaica, the seductive attire of young women passing by, and catching lobster. Occasionally, Dave and Jack slipped into Jamaican patois, which left Chance clueless.

Now, the next day, Jack and the novice lobstermen are huddling together quietly on the sand. Syncopated surf provides a steady rhythm to their chores.

"You try next one," Jack says, tossing his third trap onto a growing pile.

It's not as easy as Jack makes it look. He grunts in modest

approval of the progress Dave makes with his. Then, he watches Chance for a moment, picks up the twisted wreckage in the gringo's lap, pulls it apart, and says, "Try again."

Broad-tailed grackles squawk from the palms. Their calls sound like laughter of an unseen audience watching a TV game show.

Jack talks about lobster fishing while his hands never stop. The best time to catch is the rainy season, November through February. When the usually clear Caribbean is stirred from wind and rain, crustaceans come closer to the shore; they are "bolder." Since they are now "at the peak" of the season, these traps should soon do well.

Jack tells the story of three brothers. Two were divers weighing about "fifty kilos each." It was common for each to capture their weight in lobster within two or three days.

"The youngest brother stayed in the boat. He was the smallest. All the island knew him only as 'Dory Boy.'"

The three boys learned to catch lobster and then trade them from their father. Though rather small in stature, each had a massive chest. They had trouble finding T-shirts or even "button-up" shirts large enough to fit, so their shirts always stayed open, as Jack's does now.

"These brothers were the first to try scuba. They used the air tanks to go deeper, where the lobster are very beeg."

One difficult day near the end of the "rainy" season, the two older boys disappeared beneath the bouncing surf on a particularly deep dive. Dory Boy dropped the stone anchor to the bottom and watched their trail of bubbles from above.

"This day, the diving brothers stay too at the bottom."

Dory Boy jumped into the water and saw his brothers far away near the anchor, not moving. With no tank and no goggles, he swam the length of the anchor rope to where his brothers lay at the bottom.

"They were coiled, twisted like conchs."

Dory Boy grabbed one, took a breath from his respirator, which had fallen to the sand, then hauled his brother up the anchor line to the top. The other followed slowly behind.

"Young Dory Boy saved his brothers. They were attacked by an unknown enemy, 'Narcosis of the Deep,' dangerous, much more than cocaine. He was only ten years old. Today, men of Corn walk the island with shirts unbuttoned in honor of this 'Dory Boy.'"

Chance and Dave forget all about building traps while listening to the story. Jack's fingers never stop. He looks up, not at them, but out to the sparkling blue-green sea.

"Wow. Quite a story," Chance says, breaking a long silence.

"Well. It's a good one to know. Jack, we are looking for a dory, too. Will you be our Dory Man?"

"No," he says quickly and bends back to work. "I am too beeg."

Grackles in the palms that were quiet throughout the story squawk loudly, as if agreeing with everything the giant Jamaican has said.

MEET THE
DEANS

On Sunday, there is less noise on Corn Island's sandy streets. The overhead rustle of palms in the morning breeze seems more insistent than the day before. In the distance, surf thrums like a drum on the beach.

Forgoing their usual morning greetings, Chance and Dave head into town. As they walk in silence, an occasional passing vehicle gives the partners a "toot toot."

Near the commercial pier, families head inland toward higher points on the island, where churches wait to welcome them. They move in clusters. Little girls are dressed in bright colored frocks, and little boys, who are unusually quiet, are decked out in crisp, white shirts. Men and women walk together, herding small family flocks. All are respectfully subdued, with only grown-ups speaking in soft tones. Chance thinks something else is different. Then it strikes him. The children all wear neatly rolled socks, and everyone is wearing shoes.

The partners arrive at the Playa Coca Hotel and order breakfast. Soon Chance recognizes this is really a business meeting;

that is why they are eating at a table with a dining cloth. Dave speaks about the past week. He acknowledges that he could have done much better. However, all that is behind them now, and they are in reasonable shape considering what they've been through.

"It's been a rough week, mate. How do you feel?"

"OK..." Chance responds, feeling something heavy is about to unload.

"Well, I feel great. I'm energized. There's nothing we can change that has already happened. We have gear. Some traps. Met some people. And we'll meet more. Not sure Nelly's is where we need to be. Thought we'd take a hike to the other side of the island today and look for more permanent housing."

"Nelly's works for me."

"It's temporary. Just temporary. Need something for the long haul."

"What about a boat?"

"For now, we'll borrow—rent—from Henri."

"Not sure that's the boat we need," Chance counters. "Kind of hard to navigate a dugout in the choppy water here. We're not on the river anymore. I think we need something a bit more... seaworthy."

Chance has grown up spending summers on the Atlantic Coast, in Georgia, South Carolina, and Florida. He knows how to navigate open water and inland tributaries. He's caught shrimp with nets from a young age and waded over oyster beds in tennis shoes. He knows how to bait a line securing minnows or squid at two points on one hook. He also knows how to cast a baited line into a stiff breeze. He knows to keep an eye on accumulating clouds and get back to shore before afternoon storms roll in.

"We can use Henri's for now," says Dave, who is clearly on a roll.

"We've got other things we need to know about, like where

the lobster are, where to set the traps. God knows the traps we made yesterday aren't doing us any good at Nelly's."

"Agreed," replies Chance. "But that canoe is one heavy son of bitch. It's hard to steer. And it leaks. We need a Jon. We need a 'Jon Boat.' Or better... we need a Dory. Like the one Big Jake was talking about."

"For what we need right now, Henri's boat will suit fine. Besides... boats cost money. Our funding is a bit flat. Unless you've got some you haven't told me about, and would like a bigger share in the business."

Breakfast arrives. Chance piles fruity jelly he's never tasted before—maybe it's mango—on chunky tortillas. This whole business thing is Dave's baby. Chance has his hands full and his pocketbook committed back home. For the first time, he is having second thoughts about the whole lobster-trapping enterprise.

"More coffee?"

"No thanks."

It's a day for exploring. They set out to walk all the way around the island, which Dave assures him they can manage before lunch. Heading north, they put the wharf behind them. Easy surf glistens, laps gently, and collapses on the sand with a "whoosh."

Dave stays above the high-water line. With his creased shorts, khaki shirt, and walking boots tied at the ankle, he strides like a conqueror set on a mission. Chance dawdles, barefoot, swimsuit, T-shirt, and sneakers slung over his shoulder, picking up and examining clamshells and bits of coral. Periodically, Dave waits ahead for his partner to catch up.

They go farther along the leeward shore than they have before. Past Henri's home and family compound, the beach curves out of sight at the island's tip, where they meet the full, unblocked Caribbean breeze and watch recreational charters cruise out to sea for a day of fishing on open water. With his chin jutting out, Dave sniffs at the sea air like a retriever on the hunt.

After about a mile, they follow the beach inland toward a crease in the jungle and the syncopated tapping of hammers. On the beach, two men hover over upturned boats propped above the sand. They wear baggy trousers with rolled cuffs and loose shirts with faded tropical prints. Blond hair cascades past their shoulders. The pounding of wooden mallets ceases as Dave and Chance approach.

"Nice boats," Dave shouts out.

"Well… they've been around. How are you guys doing?"

"Not bad. I'm Dave. This is Chance. You guys look like Yanks."

"Been here for a while. Came two years ago from the States. Not seen you here before. On vacation?"

The younger of the two men goes back to hammering caulk into seams on the upturned boat. The elder speaks easily to the island newbies.

"I'm Don Dean. This is Mike, my son. Welcome to our 'Grotto.' I think it's time for a break. Don't see many visitors on this side of Corn. Kinda why we like this part. What gives with you guys?"

Dave is reluctant to discuss the reason he and Chance are here.

"Just looking around. Drove as far as we could. Then hitched a lift on a tramper. Took about two, almost three weeks."

"Nice here," adds Chance.

"Yeah. We like it. Casual. Chill. We make a little money doing what we like to do—fishing. It's laid-back here. Might be time for a smoke."

Dean leads them to a shady spot, sheltered from the breeze, and lights a hand-rolled cigarette. Seabirds wade through a small tidal stream cutting through the sand. One bird snags a shiny minnow between pincer jaws, turns toward the sea, and flies away.

At about the same time, Chance and Dave recognize a familiar smell. It's pot.

"Join me?" asks Dean, inhaling deeply through clenched teeth.

"No thanks. Taking a break." Dave shakes his head.

"Don't mind if I do. Been a while." Chance reaches out.

They sit in the shade listening to Dean talk about his business with nervous energy. He has spent a lifetime on the water but always working for someone else. He compares Corn Island to the "Wild West" during the late 1800s. He paints a romantic picture of uncharted lands, limitless waters, and a broad future for himself, his family, and anyone willing to give it a try. Dave finally confesses his motive for being here is the same.

"Great, man! Great! The more the merrier." Dean pulls hard on a second joint.

"Mike, come join us," he shouts to his son.

The younger Dean looks up, shakes his head, and continues his work caulking planks on a wooden dory. The older Dean paces in the shade. Encouraging Dave to "get busy, man," he projects a future where he, Dave, and others can build thriving businesses selling fish here on the island, then throughout the country and across Central America.

"Even, one day, all the way to the States."

The higher Dean gets on weed, the brighter the picture of the future. Finally, Dave speaks up.

"There's one big problem. What about the General? *El Presidente?*"

"Are you kidding me? He's not a problem. He's the solution. He comes here all the time. Brings a whole crowd. Boy, do they love fish, fishing, and women. Just play by his rules and it's all copacetic."

Dean takes a big pull on another joint, holds it, then convulses with a deep, rattling cough.

"How about some lunch?" he says finally.

"Thanks anyway. We're on a mission."

"Where do you guys hang out?"

"Well, we have a little cabin near the wharf."

"No... hang out?"

"We like the Fishin' Hole," Chance finally speaks out. He feels disoriented but also relaxed and strangely at home. It must be the pot.

They thank Don Dean and his son for their time. Soon Chance and Dave are back on the beach, continuing their loop of the island. The sun is now high in the sky. And the tide is much farther out, close to the coral reef.

"Ready for a bite?"

"Are you kidding? I'm starved."

"No doubt."

They complete their island loop well before noon. After lunch at the Fishin' Hole, Chance goes back to Nelly's, ending up where their day began. Dave stays at the wharf to "check on some business."

Back at the shack, Chance sees boxes and bags at the door of the previously unoccupied cabin next door. Two young men dressed in catalog versions of tropical work uniforms (laced boots, matching khaki shorts and shirts, sparkling white T-shirts peeking out at the throat, and large waterproof wristwatches with built-in compasses) go in and out of the cabin. They move with purpose, as though working by the clock.

For several minutes, Chance pretends he does not see them. Then they pause on the porch and look about. When, in unison, they eye Chance in his doorway, he smiles and waves. Each of them waves back, looking for all the world like fully grown scouts ready to salute the flag.

"Welcome to Paradise." Chance gives a sweeping gesture to the shared grounds.

"Hello. Hello."

"Hi."

Jeffrey and John are fourth-year medical students from Wisconsin. They are here on an assignment to gather data for a study of parasites and tropical diseases. The project is funded by the World Health Organization. They have come to relieve other researchers currently encamped on Corn Island's highest point, Mount Pleasant.

"That sounds dangerous, gathering poisonous samples all day," Chance says.

"Not really. We have all the right gear. Already done a lot of research," Jeff says, looking to John.

"At least we're not in Antarctica," John agrees.

"Yeah. We lucked out. Others we know really have it hard."

"Luck of the draw. But I'm sure we'll pay for it somehow. How about you?"

Chance gives the now-familiar summary of why he and Dave are here.

"That sounds cool," the two aspiring docs agree.

"Where do you eat around here? I'm sick of these protein bars."

"How 'bout some local seafood and a brew?"

"Sounds great! Let's do it."

Chance, Jeff, and John are soon tucked into a booth at the Fishin' Hole. Chance introduces his new acquaintances to owner Lyle. They slurp down buckets of shrimp and pitchers of beer.

Chance shares a few insider tips and, for the first time, feels like a true local even though he's been on Corn Island for less than a week. He watches as the familiar crowd wanders in. Music plays nonstop on the jukebox. Shadows grow long on the sandy road outside. The three split the tab. For Chance, it is an indulgence. One of the meds leaves a large tip. Together, they go outside.

"Show you around a little bit?"

"That would be great."

Chance has forgotten which is Jeff and which is John. In his mind, they are now J & J.

They walk by the Promarblu commissary, which Chance recommends for breakfast. He takes them by the Chinaman's store.

"It looks tiny, but the guy seems to have everything," he tells them.

They take a long walk on the beach. A vivid, golden sun sinks toward the treetops. The meds keep their boots tightly laced, but Chance kicks the foamy water as they walk about a mile back and forth, then return to the Fishin' Hole.

Now the joint is jumping. The patrons appear reluctant to hand the weekend back to the clock. It is as noisy as Saturday night. Peter Tosh and Bob Marley trade sets on the juke.

Chance sees Dave across the room at a noisy table, which is occupied mostly by young women. Dave slides his chair, stands up, and shakes hands with the new arrivals.

"Meet our new neighbors, Jeffrey and John."

"Pleasure," Dave shouts over the rowdy crowd. "Join us?"

"No. Thanks. It has been a very long day. Let's talk tomorrow."

"Right."

Chance, Jeffrey, and John walk back to Nelly's. After they thank their guide for the tour, everyone turns in for the night.

TWO MD WANNABES

It's been a month since Dave and Chance left their homes in the U.S., and today is going to be their first full week as lobstermen. There are no formalities or licenses necessary. Unlike their experiences crossing international borders, here, the world accepts what they say. They say they are fishermen, so they are.

Once again, both wake before dawn. Dave is the first to claim the throne for morning rituals. Chance scribbles a bit in his day book. Dave returns with slicked-back hair, smoothly shaved chin, and purposeful stride.

"Told those med students I'd give 'em a tour around the island. What's the plan for today?"

"It's Monday. Seafood boat sails back to the mainland Thursday. I intend to have product in the hold by then."

"Product?"

"Lobster, man. Tails. It's why we're here. Remember? Talked to the processing manager at Promarblu. Said he'd have room in the cooler if we had some tails to send to market."

"Wow. Good work. He'll pay us?"

"Yeah. He'll pay. Says he doesn't care how he gets them as long as they're clean and on ice. No silly inspectors to worry about down here. Says he'll pay the 'Fair Market' price. Just gotta be fresh-caught and frozen. The bigger the better."

"That's great news. When did all this happen?"

"Friday. When they were cleaning down the boats and... prepping for Saturday market. Think you were back here writing... or napping."

Chance ignores the apparent dig. Dave walks out the door as if he's late for a train.

"Let's meet for lunch at the cafeteria. Eleven or so. I'll have a better plan by then. Right now, I'm going to see about our boat."

"Sounds good. I'll be done with the meds by then."

"Hope so. It looks like they're ready to go."

Their two new neighbors are dressed and waiting on the porch. One is reading a small book; the other is staring into the trees through pocket-sized binoculars. Their creased tropical outfits seem to match. It's the cookie-cutter government-issue look. Their "research grant" includes wardrobe.

"Hungry?" asks Chance, hailing from porch to porch.

"Famished. Feels like I've been in quarantine."

"I'll be right back. Then we can go. Got business to attend to."

Chance heads around back to the shared outhouse.

"Don't fall in. You might hurt the critters down below."

"Just call it Jeffrey's petri dish."

"I think John's john might be more to the point."

One med student smacks the broad-brimmed safari cap off the head of the other.

Chance says, "Yuck." He doubts he'll ever know now which med student is which.

Soon, Chance, and J & J are seated at the Playa Coca patio.

122

Breakfast takes a while, even though all three eat quickly. Chance has learned to be satisfied with smaller portions. The two med students bring appetites accustomed to immense satisfaction. There are eggs, beans, tortillas, grilled pork, some potatoes, and even broiled fish. They drink a variety of freshly squeezed juice but little coffee. Their table requires the attention of three different servers.

"Now *that's* what I call a meal," says Jeffrey or John, leaning back in his chair contentedly and stroking a taut belly. J #1/2 belches in agreement.

"Looked like you guys haven't eaten for days."

"Not like that. At least not since Managua. Maybe Panama."

"Colón, Panama," says the other. "Now I see why everybody's so small here. They don't eat." He sops the last greasy smear from his plate.

"Let's go for a spin in our boat," says one of the J's. Chance is eager to see what they have.

The three new friends are soon walking down the charter boat dock. Seemingly knowing where they are going, the two J's lead the way to the far end of one slip, where they stop. Here a lengthy open hull boat covered with tarpaulin bobs in the harbor's chop.

"This must be it," says J #1.

"We'll know in a minute. Help me pull back the tarp," directs J #2.

They both kneel on the dock. For a moment, Chance imagines the two tending to an injured person, perhaps at the scene of an auto accident. One pulls a fore line tight to the pier; the other applies a key to a lock that keeps a heavy, custom-fit cover secure across the top of the boat. The lock is released, and a steel cable relaxes. Together, they pull the tarp up and back, fore and aft. They climb into the craft and fold up the heavy cloth, and the man up front stows it beneath the bow.

Still on the dock, Chance examines a tidy, pale blue, open

hull, fiberglass boat rocking beside the pier. It's about twenty feet long with a bow cleat pointing upward. There are four bench seats on the craft, one directly behind a sophisticated cockpit with windshield. Gunwales bulge from each side.

Two forty horsepower outboard motors, like the one Dave and Chance lugged all the way from Virginia, are mounted side by side on the stern. A large portable fuel tank is attached to the motor with an identical spare nearby. Numerals are painted on the front of the boat next to an emblem with the letters *UW*. On the boat's rear, the word "Cheesehead" is painted in a curve resembling a smile.

Chance is stunned. It's a beautiful boat—a far cry from the dugouts or plank-on-frame double-enders surrounding it. And it looks barely used, like something in a catalog.

"Think it'll crank?" one J asks the other.

"Only one way to find out. A guy named Jorge checked it over yesterday. The crew on the Mount says it runs just fine. They call it a panga."

"Panda?"

"No, ass. Panga, after the fish."

"Never seen one."

"They're kinda new. Designed for the locale."

The motor sputters, then roars to life after three pulls on the cord. Now they have to shout above the noise.

"All aboard," yells Skipper J.

"Let's do this. Which way, Chance? Lead us out. You know these waters," says the other, putting on a faded baseball cap with a UW emblem.

Nothing could be further from the truth, but Chance will give it a try. He feels at home, barefoot in this well-kept, sturdy open craft.

"Stay in the channel. Just watch the buoys."

In minutes, they are out of the oil-streaked harbor, heading for a wide break in the coral reef, then out to sea. Chance directs them south, along the island's coast, then north after a wide, swooping 180-degree jibe. He drinks in the sea air and even relishes the fine spray caused by the bouncing prow. Skipper J appears to have the throttle wide open. There is no way to hear someone speak.

The boat speeds out to open water. Just beyond the coral reef, J at the helm abruptly decelerates, causing "Cheesehead" to bobble in its wake. All three look out over the uninterrupted Caribbean, a wrinkled, undulating reflection of the baby blue sky above.

They find a bag with masks and fins and take turns jumping and swimming in the water. During the morning, the J's tell Chance about their upcoming stay on Corn and how today is the only full day for them to "get acquainted" with the island. Knowing it is small, they push to see as much as they can. Chance directs them to several spots he's seen only from shore.

They take turns in the water, but recent rains have made the water cloudy. The two young researchers are disappointed by the visibility but not by their access and views of the island from offshore.

They cruise all around the island, Mount Pleasant, where their "station" is located. They tell Chance he must visit them there soon. It's known as a historic hideaway for pirate treasure, "So bring a strongbox when you come. No telling what we might find."

Chance shows them Long Bay and Don Dean's "Grotto," where Mike Dean interrupts his boatyard work for a broad wave and a smile. They pause at the north end of the island and discuss the distance across open water to Little Corn, rapidly concluding there's no time to visit it today, "...but definitely before we leave."

J & J drop Chance off at the commercial wharf near dusk, in time to meet Dave, who has just settled in behind a frosty cold one at the Fishin' Hole. Dave talks about his day finishing traps and touring productive "lobster holes" with Mike Dean. Chance talks about his day with the med students. Then Dave tells Chance of his plan to meet a new friend called Pansy for dinner, and that there is no need for Chance to come along.

Chance ends his day much as it began. He walks back to Nelly's. He spends the evening writing letters, reading, and reflecting on his morning with J #1 and J #2. He has a quiet dinner alone from provisions already on hand, then sits outside on the small porch.

As night falls, Chance goes to the beach to walk the shore. He returns to a quiet place he has found toward the south end of the island, where apparently few people go. He sits on a high rise of sand, looking out as the sun exhausts itself behind a cloud bank. The quiet sea turns to liquid silver, then molten lead, and, finally, it gains a rosy hue as final strands of sunlight dim.

"Good night, World," he says.

Walking back to Nelly's compound, Chance notices phosphorescent sparkles in the timid waves. Are these tiny reflections of the moon that the crab, shrimp, lobster, and fish enjoy every night? Or are they something different?

Chance wishes he had someone, the right partner, with whom to discuss this matter. He falls asleep almost instantly with the crescent moon hanging, seemingly suspended, in the window just above his head.

CAMP EL PRESIDENTE

"I found the boat we need. Seriously, I found the boat. Or at least one just like it."

Outside the large open window, Big Corn Island dock traffic rushes by just like the day before. Like every day, except Sunday. It's late Tuesday morning and the early breakfast rush is over at the Promarblu factory commissary. Dave polishes off another hearty breakfast as Chance sips coffee and then continues his pitch.

"It's called a panga. It'll fit your motor just right. Cuts straight through the water. Any kind of water: calm, choppy, big breakers, all of it. It has a wide, flat bottom and plenty of room for fish. Just what you—just what we—need. I rode on one yesterday with those Wisconsin guys. It's sweet."

Dave swims back slowly from his own private thoughts.

"It's sweet, I tell you... *sweeeet*."

Older customers now shuffle into the commissary. They order coffee, sit at familiar tables, mostly alone, nodding as other grayhairs pass by. Soon, when the breakfast shift ends, there will be discounts, beans, grilled corn, and bits of leftover fish for half price. These are retired dockhands holding creased and faded ID cards with shaky fingers. Often, they get breakfast for free. None are women.

"We've got a boat. Remember?" Dave answers curtly. "It's on loan, from Henri. We'll pay him when we can. Which ain't right now. Or did you and your new pals dig up a little Blackbeard treasure yesterday?"

"Unfortunately, no. But we did get an invite to their lab on Mount Pleasant."

"Lovely. Don't forget the sunscreen."

Chance has already told Dave all about his day with the medical students. So now he talks mostly about the boat.

"I've seen 'em. Even been on one or two. And I know they cost a bit," Dave concedes.

"Probably. But I tell you, it's what we need. Flat on the bottom. You can stand with no problem. The bow is raised and pointed so it cuts through the surf like a knife. You can push it right off the beach."

"We got a boat. And it's time we got in it."

Back at Henri's boatyard, quiet adults in the yard welcome the gringos when they return. A stack of curious young faces peers through the front porch screen. Dave distributes trinkets for the kids. He offers plantain and breadfruit to the mother, and, for Henri, a small U.S. flag. Then the gringos retrieve their gear from the storage closet behind Henri's house. All is in order. Nothing has been disturbed.

They load their motor on a cart and pull it like mules across the sand. Henri and his brothers have one dugout already in the water, pointing seaward. Dave mounts the motor on the rear of the other one with a little help. The prop remains elevated at an angle above the sand. Seasoned seaworthy hands hold the boat steady as it bobs in the surf, prancing like a Derby contender at the starting gate.

"The weather is kind today," observes Henri.

"You are kind to trust us with your boat," Dave quickly answers back.

"This boat will bring you home. It always does."

"How much do we owe you?"

"We will see when you return."

Again, Chance is moved by the generosity of the people here. He climbs aboard and moves to the front. A long paddle is waiting for him there. Dave steps to the rear and sits at the stern, another paddle at his feet. Henri and his brothers shove them off. They push the boat hard beyond the breakers while Dave pumps fuel to the motor, flicks a switch, and pulls on the starter cord. The third pull is the charm.

Two hundred yards out, before they reach the reef, Dave banks hard to starboard. He sets a course parallel to the shore and heads north. Chance stows his paddle and leans forward.

"You swim, right?" Chance shouts behind him.

"Like a porpoise," Dave grins. "Grew up in Jamaica. You're the city boy. Can you?"

It's a joke they share, indicating both are in a good mood. In roughly ten minutes, Dave slows the motor, causing the vessel to lurch in its wake, then executes a 90-degree turn back to the beach where Trapper Jack sits in the sand. Soon, Chance pulls the prow ashore. Dave kills the engine, jumps out, and helps pull the heavy boat's nose out of the water.

Jack watches, sitting in the sand before his shed. There is a pile of traps behind him. Some are long and funnel-shaped. Others are round with flat bottoms. Most are made of woven wire, but there are a few rustic ones made only of twigs.

"G'mornin', Mon."

"Yo," Jack answers, not looking up.

Dave is eager to get underway but feigns patience as Jack's thick fingers weave and bob through the wire. Jack reaches to his tangle of hair, pulls out a nail, executes an intricate maneuver on the trap, and returns the nail to its nest. Chance wonders if the muscle-bound Jamaican sleeps with nails in his hair.

"We're here for some traps, Mon."

The trapper makes no sound. He stares at his lap and stays quiet for a long time. Chance counts waves lapping on the sand without looking up. Jack points over his shoulder to traps behind.

Dave turns smartly in place and marches to the pile. For several minutes, he inspects every one. Chance stands near Jack, facing the dazzling turquoise sea. With water so clear, he sees broad outlines of dark vegetation on the reef forty feet below. When waves rise, he looks straight through them, seeing clouds against the sky. While studying the constantly evolving watercolor before him, he pulls out a stack of córdoba notes held flat by a girl's hair clip. He fingers the bills without looking, counting to confirm their number.

Dave puts a trap beneath each arm. They are about six feet long and sag on each end as he walks back to face the quiet trap builder.

"I would like these. How much?"

Jack lifts his head slowly and peers out to sea without looking at Dave. Finally, he speaks.

"You have picked my best. Every trap is different. Those two will 'keel' the langos. I made them just yesterday when I was at my best."

"I see. How much for these two traps?"

"Thirty cords. Each. Sixty for two."

Dave takes a long pause. He, too, examines the waves. "I will give fifty for two."

"Sixty."

Chance hands Jack three twenty-córdoba bills.

The trapper says, "Thanks," and tucks the bills in his shirt without counting.

The exchange is complete. During the bargaining, neither Jack nor Dave makes eye contact.

Back in the boat, the rookie seamen make ready once again to shove off. Before they leave, "Chance... mate... dude..." says Dave, "Don't ever do that again. It's not... it's just not... genuine." Dave speaks more like a teacher than a frustrated business partner.

"Well... I get it. I felt awkward stepping in, but... how long would that have taken?"

"A while."

"I didn't feel like we had the time. Look at the sun."

"I know. But that's not the point. That's not how business is done here. And now you have permanently fixed the price of our traps for the future. There's a reason these things take time."

Dave turns to tend to the motor, which cranks with the first pull. Now Chance must shout.

"Sorry, man, got ahead of myself. Thought I was helping out. Anyway... we still gotta get these puppies in the water," Chance says, pointing to the traps, "and we don't know where to put them or how."

"That's why we're going to Dean's."

Dave opens up the motor, and the dugout plows further north, skirting the coral reef about a quarter mile offshore. Soon Little Corn Island appears in the distance. The wind has picked up, and there is serious chop as they approach the channel between the two islands. They cruise for several minutes. Dave scouts the beachfront, looking for familiar markers. Chance looks too. He sees a crease on the shore and points it out.

"I think that's it—where we met Dean. I think that's the 'Grotto.'"

"I think you're right. Let's go see."

Slowing the boat, Dave follows a dark channel to shore. Soon, behind a tall, sandy outcropping, they see boats overturned and two figures tending to dory hulls. A large charter fishing boat is moored to a buoy in the tight cove. Dave heads slowly toward shore, grabbing the workers' attention with the sound of the engine. They recognize Don and Mike Dean.

Dave rides the crest of a small wave, guns the motor one last time, and then kills it. Crouching over the stern, he pulls a pin and tips the engine forward just as the prop is about to make contact with the sand. Chance leaps out barefoot with a rope in hand that's tied to the front of the boat. The canoe grinds to a sandy halt.

"Knew you'd be back," yells Don Dean.

"Yeah, you were right. Maybe a little sooner than we thought. We're looking for a little advice," shouts Dave.

"Come on up. I've got plenty. That's about all I've got these days." Dean grins and helps pull the boat up the beach. "Hey, Mike. Come give us a hand," Dean calls out to his son.

Mike Dean heads down to the boat. Together, they pull the heavy canoe mostly out of the water, making it look like a helpless sea creature washed ashore after a storm. Don Dean examines their cargo in the well of the boat.

"Nice traps. Make 'em yourself?"

"I wish. Not that crafty yet. Jack the Jamaican made 'em. Look good to you?"

"Look great. You went to the right guy. Best on the island. Did he talk your ears off?"

"Not exactly."

"Where you gonna drop 'em?"

"Well. We don't know. Maybe you could give us some tips. Course, nothing that would hurt your trade."

"Don't worry about that. Whadda they say... 'Lotta fish in the sea'? Goes for lobster, too. Let's go up to the house. Look at a map. You guys look thirsty. What up, Chancey? Feeling lucky?"

Dean's partner, Jenny, a sturdy, shapely women with a ponytail, has heard the sounds of arrival and most of the exchange from the house. When Chance, Dave, Dean, and Mike enter, there is beer in a bucket on the table. There's also a large bowl of dried plantain. Something smells very good in the kitchen, where popping sounds come from a skillet. The music of the Doors sets a hipster tone.

Over lunch, Dean tells his guests about doing research on the Caribbean and a place he'd never heard about called Corn Island, Nicaragua, and about how he ended up at the "Grotto."

"Getting down here was a bitch. Not the trip—that was pretty smooth—but making it all legal. Bringing a boat. I had no idea. Now I'm here, I'm staying. Got this place. Got my team. Two boats now. Room to expand. Who knows, maybe we can do a little business together. It's really easy to get going here... as long as—"

"That would be perfect. We just need to know where to start," Dave cuts in.

"It's really easy to get going here. Just stay out of the way of the Big Guy."

"Big Guy?"

"You know, *El Presidente*. He and his family come here a lot. They own Promarblu, the fish factory, and just about everything else. Play by their rules and you'll do fine. When they're here, just lay low."

"The Big Guy?" Chance asks again.

"C'mon... you know, the *Generalissimo, El Presidente*. He comes here all the time. And so does his huge family."

"Ah."

"They run the island when they're here, just like everything else in the country."

"Oh, yeah."

The conversation runs into a total word block. All are silent for several seconds. Dean stretches, yawns, rubs his belly, then gets up.

"Mike can show you how it's done. Grab some bait out of the box. I'm beat. Talk more later."

The rest of the day is spent on the water with Mike. It's crowded in the dugout, but they cover a lot of water. Mike directs them to a spot near the "Grotto," a breeding bank for langosta. He shows how to bait the traps with smelly chicken parts and maneuver the boat in order to drop traps to just the right depth, and how much line to leave between the trap and buoy.

They tour other locations near the Deans' home. Mike talks about his work with the "family fishing business" and how much better fishing of all types is here than in mainland Florida and the Keys.

After about an hour, the trap placement exercise is over.

"Got your bearings?" Mike asks.

"Not really. Been looking for a map. Can't seem to find one," says Dave.

"Not easy to find. People don't need 'em here."

Mike points out the highest point on the island, near where they bob. Thick forest rises about two hundred feet above the shore, and there's a radio tower at the peak. "That's Mount Pleasant. You can see it from almost anywhere. If you get turned around on the island while on the water, find 'the Mount' and you can find your way home... or wherever you're trying to get to," young Dean explains.

"Oh, yeah. The medical students were talking about it. They called it 'the Lab.'"

"I've never been up there. Sounds creepy to me. The medical laboratory. Maybe they're making a third-world Frankenstein. Who knows? I don't care. Anyway... it's fenced off, all around. *No Entrada*. Mostly because it backs up the Big Guy's beach house, Casa Tachito. Lotta big hombres strutting around with ugly machine guns." This gets both Chance and Dave's complete attention. They look at each other wide-eyed.

"Wow. For real?"

"For real."

"What goes on there?

"The General owns a big chunk of land up there. Runs all the way down to the sea. His papa, the first General, owned it before that. Story goes, the U.S. purchased the Mount when they were planning to build another canal, like the one in Panama, in the early 1900s. That never happened. But the gringos liked the perch. So they kept it."

"So the United States used to own that mountain? Just the mountain? In the middle of the island? That seems odd."

"Like Guantanamo in Cuba," Dave kicks in.

"Maybe. I don't know. Not really my thing. The U.S. still controls it. Clear view all around. Great reception for radio and such. Good place to keep an eye on things all across the Caribe."

They all focus on the mountain, where radio towers finger the clouds. Chance imagines the crackle of radio signals, voices of military spies trading info about comings and goings all around the beautiful Caribbean. Must have been frantic during the Cuban Missile Crisis. Maybe these innocent lobstermen are being tracked by spooks right now.

"But the U.S. government ended up selling the beachfront to Big Guy's family for next to nothing. Presidents here are known for sweetheart deals. What's good for the president is suitable for the people of Nicaragua."

There is no expression of irony or conviction on Mike Dean's face as he scans the horizon.

"What about the treasure?" Dave wants to know.

"Treasure? What treasure?"

"Last time I was here, somebody told me that mountain was made out of gold. Built by pirates."

"There haven't been any pirates for centuries."

"Really? Who lives in that fancy palace in Managua?"

"Oh, him. He's not a pirate. He's just a modern business-man, Anastasio 'Tachito' Somoza Debayle. We call him *Señor Presidente*. Learned most of his craft in the States. Go figure. Wanna see his beach house? Go that way."

Dave engages the motor. They roar off against the chop—the little craft swings toward the open Caribbean, in the direction Mike Dean points. Soon he signals to slow down and, with the tide coming in, Mike directs Dave closer to shore. They see a small cluster of buildings and an empty gravel road. A white-framed bell tower rises above the trees.

Here at the northernmost tip of the island, there are no more houses or even huts. In the distance, as the island gives way to the open sea, there is a long dock with a guardhouse at each end. A man with a weapon steps out on the pier. He looks at them through binoculars, then waves them away.

"That's it. That's as far as we can go. Make a nice, gentle about-face and let's get out of here."

Dave executes a slow 180-degree turn. He sets their course back the way they came over the mottled pastel water.

"What just happened?" Chance finally asks.

"That was the president's dock, and that's as warm a greeting as you're gonna get there."

"What were all the guns for?"

"Standard issue. There's always some bigwig there. Just cooling their heels. It's one of *Presidente*'s local headquarters. Ever heard of Camp David in the U.S.? It's like that. I hear there are lots all over Nic. The family's been collecting fancy homes for years."

"So is the president there... like on vacation?"

"No, if he were there, we wouldn't have gotten that close."

Dave opens the throttle full wide. In fifteen minutes, they

reach the "Grotto." They agree to meet Mike later at the Fishin' Hole.

They return the boat to Henri's and unload their gear but leave the motor mounted. Dave asks Henri how much they owe him for the day's rental.

He answers, "Nuttin' now," and tells Dave that they can pay after their first catch.

They thank him again for this generosity and invite Henri and his brothers to join them later for a beer in town.

Henri thanks them but says, "We no drink the cerveza. Must keep the mind and heart clear for 'the Message.'"

A short time later, it's noisy at the Fishin' Hole. Dave, Chance, and Mike agree it's been a good day.

"We've learned a lot, Mike. Let's celebrate," Dave says, slamming three frosty bottles on the table.

"Sounds good to me," Chance agrees.

"Here on the island, the people always celebrate with 'Rundown,'" Mike says.

"Rundown? What's that?"

"It's a stew. A seafood stew made with coconut milk. Kinda sweet. Tastes better than it sounds. Particularly with plenty of rum."

"Let's give it a try."

Soon they are slurping down what their server calls "rondón" from bowls the size of basins. The stew is hearty and satisfying, filled with lobster, fish, and crab swimming with cassava, breadfruit, and yams in a thick coconut broth. Onion, garlic, and chili make the dish more spicy than sweet. They dip pieces of fried plantain in their bowls until there's not a drop left. A bottle of rum helps it all go down nicely.

Dave takes the bottle and empties the remains into three glasses.

"How about a toast for our day—and our new friend," says Dave with a smirk.

"Sounds good to me. I'm ready," Chance says, looking at Mike.

"Let's see if I can remember... OK. Here's one from back home, in Jamaica...

"On the chest of a barmaid named Gail

"Were tattooed the prices of ale. And on her behind

"For the sake of the blind

"Was the same information in Braille."

Chance gives Mike a critical look. They both sip their drinks.

"OK. Here's one. Maybe a little easier to swallow..." Chance looks at Mike, then back at Dave. He salutes each with his glass.

"There are good ships, and there are wood ships,

"But the best ships are friendships."

"Nice, Chance. Mike, you got one?"

"Yeah. I got one. I don't know if it fits."

"Lay it on, if you feel like."

"May you live as long as you want. And never want as long as you live."

Each fisherman drains his glass and bangs it down on the table.

Out on the sandy road, as the sun sets like a golden amulet behind a parade of clouds, they agree to meet the next day to scout more locations for setting traps.

Then Mike heads back along the beach to the "Grotto." Dave strikes out toward town because he has "an errand to run." Chance takes the familiar path through the jungle back to Nelly's shack. He hasn't mentioned it, but now that it is after midnight, it is his birthday. What a way to begin his twenty-fifth year.

DIVING WITH MIKE

E arly the next day, the three young seamen load up. Dave sits at the helm. Mike leans into the wind over the prow. Chance balances the craft by sitting in the boat's middle.

They head out beyond the western reef, then north, running parallel to the shore. It's easy to see the profile of the island this far out. Dave opens the throttle full tilt and they all hold on tight against the chop. Mount Pleasant looms behind to their right, and coming into view onshore is a green, rolling space decorated with regular white markers Chance has not noticed before.

"Have you been to the cemetery yet?"

"What?" Chance yells out to Mike.

"The cemetery. Have you been to the cemetery yet?"

"No. It's not high on our agenda. Hope I don't have a need to."

"It's near our place. I like it because we are close. Hardly anybody goes there... I like it mostly because of that."

Dave can't hear them at the back. He keeps staring forward as Mike continues.

"People say the 'spooks' will keep you up at night. And I happen to know they do," Mike says.

It is an odd comment, but Chance doesn't pursue it. "This whole trip is odd," he thinks.

In minutes, they are approaching the "drop zone" they used the day before. It has been about twenty-four hours, and sea conditions are nearly the same. There is an easterly breeze and mild chop, and the water is slightly murky. Mike acts as a guide over these familiar waters. He signals Dave to slow down. Then he throws his palm straight in the air. "Stop!" Dave slips the motor into neutral, and then kills it.

They bob above thirty feet of clear seawater as a gang of black-capped petrels flies by. Chance drops anchor. Mike strips down to cutoffs, then makes a neat portside dive. He rises to the surface, treading water.

"Hand me a mask, will ya?" he shouts.

Chance grabs a diving mask and throws it to Mike. After putting it on, Mike looks below for about a minute, and then looks up.

"OK. I see the traps. I'll be back."

Executing a crisp surface dive, he disappears below. The two would-be trappers watch Mike's vanishing point intently. Two minutes pass by, then Chance and Dave look at each other. The loudest sound is the slap of waves against the side of the boat.

"Hey! Look at this!"

About fifty yards farther out to sea, they see Mike's head bobbing at the surface. His arms are raised high. In each hand, he holds a lobster.

"Come get me," he shouts.

In very little time, the dugout is rocking beside the diver. Chance grabs one langosta, puts it in a burlap bag, and then grabs the second. There's no problem handling the lobster because they are clawless. As soon as Mike hands the second one to Chance, he pushes off from the boat.

"I'll be back. There's more."

Chance drops the anchor on the opposite side of the boat from where Mike is. Dave keeps the motor running in neutral. Again, they wait. Mike is out of sight for another minute, then two.

"Man, that guy's got some lungs."

"I guess they come with the job," agrees Dave.

Mike pops up again, this time much closer to the boat. He has only one lobster, but it is nearly twice as large as the first two. He hands it to Chance, who regards it suspiciously. Mike swims to the canoe's rear and hands up his mask, then Dave helps their new friend climb aboard.

"That one's a whopper."

"Yeah. It must be Daddy. Let's get back to the house. My dad will show you how to take care of your catch."

Later, back at the "Grotto," Dave takes a victory lap. There are congratulations and thanks all around. Jenny brings out a bucket with beer and sets it in the sand beside the boat. Dean tells Dave and Chance that they have "passed their audition." He shows them how to prepare the two smaller lobster for market but insists they eat the big one now.

"It's bad luck not to eat your first catch of the day, like spitting in the eyes of Neptune. I'll take the other two, put 'em on ice, then take them down to Promarblu tomorrow. Looks like you two have the touch. We're going to get along just fine. Right, Mike?"

Mike says nothing but grins beneath a shaggy blond forelock. Jenny takes the big lobster into the house.

"You guys, get your boat to where it belongs, then get back here in a hurry. We'll have what we call a 'Seafood Feast.' Not sure what we'll have, but bring an appetite."

"Sounds good."

Dave and Chance shove the boat off with Don and Mike Dean's help. They motor around to Henri's, pull the canoe up on the beach, and put motor and gear in the shed.

Then they walk back to the "Grotto," where Dean and Mike are lounging deep in the shade of magnolia, pine, and palm trees beside a round table made from a large cable spool. There's beer on ice in a tub. It's early afternoon, and the new lobstermen are now starving. Soon Jenny joins them, bearing a platter of boiled shrimp with the large lobster, which is now pink, resting on top.

Chance feels right at home. This late lunch/early dinner reminds him of crab boils back home in coastal Georgia. Messy, hands-on seafood meals enjoyed fresh from nets, traps, and fishing lines are always viewed as part sustenance and part celebration. Almost sacred. He remembers children at family events seated in strollers slurping raw oysters from shells and asking for "mo'."

After a couple of hours sipping beer and snapping shells, laziness seeps into everyone's bones. Chance and Dave thank Dean and Jenny for the meal. They rise to leave. Mike walks with them down to the shore. He shakes hands with both and thanks them. His gesture goes on a little too long with each, almost as if he is making a joke.

"Thanks for everything," says Dave.

"No, thank you," answers Mike.

"What are you talking about? You did all the work."

"No. I mean it," says Mike. "You guys have shown me a lot. Probably more than you know." He shakes both of their hands again, for the third time.

"Well, we still have lots to learn. Let's do it again. Soon."

"We'll see," says Mike. He walks quickly to the house.

The partners turn back toward the wharf as breezes hum through the trees.

"That was odd."

"A bit."

"Guess he doesn't see many people like us. Back to the hut?"

"No. I've got another stop to make. You go ahead."

"Pansy?"

Dave looks a bit startled.

"Perhaps. Told her I'd look her up today. Now might be a good time."

"Good luck... see you later. Maybe for dinner?"

"Maybe. I'll certainly need to freshen up."

"Right."

Dave veers off into the trees. Chance heads back to the shack. He's eager to be alone and maybe write a letter or two. Late afternoon light gives each tree and tall bush a unique personality; they look as if, at any second, they could walk or talk.

"Too many cartoons," Chance says to himself.

The lobster catch with Mike is a considerable boost. It confirms Dave's plan for a successful business, and joining the Deans for family dinner seems to be a stamp of their approval. Despite the fatigue of a full day, Chance is energized and bristling with anticipation.

There is no moon in the sky. The stars stand out brighter than they did the previous night. He recognizes clusters that radiate, even twinkle, for attention. Orion the Hunter shines in the south, the brightest, easiest constellation to find.

As always, the Hunter chases seven sisters. Why can't he stop them with his large shield and mighty sword? What about that glowing belt? Why are his dogs always behind him, barking at his heels? Why don't they get out ahead, like faithful retrievers? And there, in the West, waiting, watching, is Aquarius, the Water Bearer.

How appropriate that, on this birthday, all the world should be racing toward Aquarius. Will Orion ever catch up with him? Does it matter? Only time will tell, and these stars have all the time in this world and the next.

However, the birthday boy has a limited supply and so must use it wisely. He has made a decision. Early the next day, he will tell Dave that he is planning to leave Corn Island as soon as he can. He has accomplished what he set out to do here, and now it's time to move on. The news will no doubt meet a stormy reception.

TIME FOR ONE
TO DEPART

The breaking day paints a warm glow on the hardwood planks in the shack. Chance writes a quick note still lying in his bunk: "Getting coffee at Playa Coca." He leaves it on the floor and steps silently out into a sea-scented breeze.

He grabs a table at the edge of the porch at Hotel Playa Coca, which has now become their business meeting spot. He orders coffee and a sweet bun. Wharf traffic is already well underway. Today will be a busy one. It's Thursday, departure day for the cargo ship loaded with fruit, fish, and passengers heading to Bluefields, Rama, and beyond.

Dave appears sooner than Chance expects. They each grunt "Morning" to the other. The jaunty Jamaican, looking particularly dapper, orders a large breakfast. Chance asks for a coffee refill, knowing he will be charged for the second, and notes that the "bottomless cup" is an American tradition not observed here in a country where coffee grows.

They watch the morning rush, and Chance wonders if the two little lobster caught the day before really will make it to the mainland. They sit quietly for several minutes, then Chance speaks up.

"Got something to tell ya," Chance says.

"OK..."

"It's time for me to head back. Back home. To the States."

Dave takes a long gulp from his cup. He looks out at the world, the sky, the jungle, and the people pouring toward the dock.

"Thought yesterday might change your mind."

"It was a good day."

"Catching those lobsters with Mike answered a lot of questions. We can do this thing."

"Yep. We learned a lot."

Dave's breakfast arrives. Chance puts a hand over his cup and shakes his head.

"We... can do this thing," Dave says again. "We... but not me alone. I need a partner."

"You got one. What about Miss Pansy?"

"Funny. You know that's not what I mean. I need a business partner."

"We both know the plan was always for me to help you get here. Get set up. I think you've done that. It's amazing what you have accomplished."

"But I'm broke."

"Me too. I'm hoping for good news from my bank back home every time I go to the PO. Nothing yet."

"But we are on the brink. We are about to break out."

"I think you're right. But I'm not your guy. Mike is the guy you need."

"You hear those grad school chimes ringing again, don't you?"

"That's part of it."

Dave loads a tablespoon of butter on a large slice of bread.

"When you thinking about heading out?" he asks, biting down.

"Soon as I can."

"Well, I guess the sooner, the better."

Chance puts more than enough córdobas on the table for his share and gets ready to leave. He's been around Dave long enough to know that this conversation is over.

"Guess I'll go over to the post office. Should be open by now. Are you looking for anything?"

"Not unless it's addressed to Kipling."

"I'll ask."

The frenzy at the commercial wharf has mostly subsided. This week's cargo ship is soon to depart. Passengers with bulging bags inch up the ramp. A man, wearing shorts, a T-shirt, and sandals but an official-looking cap, collects tickets. The sun is high, and everyone is looking for shade.

Near the Promarblu commissary, Chance leans in at a window marked "Dockmaster." A man he has seen before but never met stands at a desk sorting cords and U.S. dollar bills. His lips bounce as he counts and separates the money into colorful stacks. There is no cash register or calculator in sight.

He wraps rubber bands around wads of money, drops them into a canvas bag on the floor, secures the bag with a lock, and kicks it under a desk. He makes notes in a ledger with a pencil stub he pulls from behind an ear. There is no wasted movement. Now, propping his lanky frame on the desk, he sends Chance a wide smile.

"So how may I help you, Mistah?"

"I'm looking to catch a ride on a boat. Back to Bluefields."

"Sorry. But you just missed that one. No more seats. Leaves in—" He looks at the boat through the glass. "—I'd say in about an hour. But I'm not the captain."

"When's the next one?"

"Next week. Same day. Same time. Thursday." Chance twists his lips from side to side, deep in thought.

"What's the hurry, Mon? You already caught all the lobster in the sea?"

Again he is reminded there are no secrets on the island.

"Not quite. Just started yesterday. And we had some luck. But that's why I came to Corn—to get the fishing started with my mate. Now that part of the job is done, and I need to get back to the States."

Chance cringes as he hears himself speaking like Dave. Back home, he would never call a friend a mate. That's what monkeys do. And parents. He's also recently heard himself call a trip "a journey" and was slightly appalled. Journeys are what happen in books, fairy tales about knights, or maybe astronauts. He has pointedly resisted calling his machete a "cutlass." For Chance, a cutlass is a car made back in the States.

"Then you deserve to celebrate. It's Thursday. Little Friday, my friend. Time to kick back and enjoy. The ladies will all be out tonight. This weekend is big. With special guests. There will be much baseball on the field. And Saturday is the market."

"Sounds good. But I need to head back."

"Well. There is always LANICA… the plane. It is sure to come tomorrow with the bank. There may still be a seat on board for you."

"Don't think I can afford it just now."

"I know, Mon. The airplane is expensive. And the plane is small. But you are small."

"Thanks for reminding me."

The gringo turns away and steps into the street.

"There's one more thing you could try, Mon," the dock-master calls out. "Maybe you could catch a ride."

Chance stops. He comes back to the window and speaks through the small, round opening there.

"You know somebody going to Blue?"

"Not right now. But you can never tell. There is always traffic on the water. And this will be a big weekend. Stay near the dock. Watch for people who live on the Main who have come to Corn for the festivity."

The tall dockmaster steps through the door, locks it, and squints at the high noon sun. Horn blasts scream across the wharf. Deckhands loosen mooring lines and draw them back on board. More shrill blasts fill the air—engines roar to life. Black smoke pours from stacks against a brilliant sky. The calm, transparent water becomes a cauldron of bubbles and foam behind the ship to Bluefields as it pulls away from the dock.

"You may be surprised if you stay near the dock. This ship is leaving early, but I am not surprised. The tide slips away and the captain knows that now is time to leave. That is the reason he is a captain. There is a reason behind everything, good and bad, even evil."

As the ship pulls away, Chance wonders if the dockmaster is giving him good news or a warning. He feels alone and now a bit small.

"You just need to know where to look. Good luck to you, my friend. *Bonne chance, mon ami.*"

Chance does not feel particularly lucky just now, as he watches the cargo ship pass Rocky Point, leaving only a foam trail as it heads west back to Bluefields.

Returning to Nelly's compound, Chance hears a syncopated "whop, whop, whop" coming from a cluster of shade. An elderly man sits on the ground before a wooden stump, a machete rising and falling to the rhythm of the "whops." Chance stops to watch.

"Bonjour."

"*Bonjou,* Mr. Chance."

"May I watch?"

The man pauses and looks up. He is bald, and his face is as creased as a well-worn purse. Sinews across his chest, shoulders, and thin arms glisten with effort. The pale soles of his feet rise and lean away from each other like tiny tombstones. He wears only baggy shorts.

"This sand here is as much for you as me."

Chance sits as the old man continues to work. For several minutes, he carves and shaves a long cylinder of hardwood, transforming it from a crude club into a graceful handle, maybe for an ax. The man pauses for a critical examination of his work. Birds caw and flutter unseen in the nearby brush.

"That's really quite lovely," offers Chance.

"Time may make it so. It is not like my Pop's. My father. He was the genius with a blade."

"Looks lovely to me. Surely you are a master carver."

The man rubs the bare wood with steel wool, at first roughly, then gently, coaxing a more graceful shape out of his work. Chance watches, mentally absorbing the man's technique.

"Your father. He lived here? On Corn Island?"

"Yes. And his mother was from Corn. But his father came from over the water. His father was a trader."

The man speaks with reverence. His grandfather came from Antigua, but his grandmother was from an indigenous "nation" of residents here on Corn Island. The man speaks as though he is addressing a large gathering, as though he has done this many times before.

Nelly, who has been handwashing clothes across the yard, joins the two men. She chimes in with the story of her family. The tales of two families merge and weave a tapestry that is the history of Corn Island.

Chance learns that before the Black Creole people of the Caribbean arrived, native tribes lived here. These were the first residents, neither Spanish nor Creole speakers. And for decades,

Corn Island was controlled by pirates, until the British took over. Seafarers claimed large properties, which were divided by stones hand-stacked into walls.

"There. Over there. You can see one of the walls." Nelly points to a collapsed mound of coral beneath thick leaves.

One day, Queen Victoria granted freedom to all Caribbean people, including those on Corn Island. That was when locals built up the copra trade, which remains essential even now, nearly a century later. There was also an iron mill, which can still be seen.

During the time when the canal was being built in Panama, Americans came to Corn, but they were mostly concerned with the mainland, Granada, León, and Managua. Except for occasional fishers and treasure seekers, Americans left the island alone. And now the island belongs to the people of the island, both historians conclude. Chance is a bit skeptical.

"And now we are a free people. As free as the sea," says Nelly.

"What about your government? What about *El Presidente?*"

Nelly and the old man look at each other. She shrugs. He is silent.

"He comes here like you. To breathe the free air of the sea."

"And to eat the lobster," the master carver smiles.

"Yes... the lobster. And all the rest. He brings his family. He has a home here. Like we do. And, like him, we all eat the gifts of the sea. His family, like ours, will come forever. Always in peace and always with many córdobas."

"He will come here soon. Maybe you will meet him while you are here, Mr. Chance."

Back at the shack, Chance regrets the years of disrespect and dishonor he has shown to his family's history and all those before him whose name he shares. And he wonders how much Nelly and the old man really believe what they say and how well they understand the current shifting sands of politics in Nicaragua. Will revolution someday touch down like a plane—or a plague—on Corn Island?

Time to sleep.

GRIM NEWS

The next day, before dawn, Chance walks down to the edge of the surf, which is lit up with fluorescent foam, like something unreal from a stage set or a cartoon. He sits in the sand and looks out to sea. There is a vague glow on the horizon where the sun will soon rise. He feels that if he watches the day begin, he has a better chance of owning it. One must see at least one sunrise at any location to feel part of the local population.

His body has begun to absorb the internal clock that so many have here on Corn Island, a place with no watches, only eternal cycles of day and night, hope and loss, life and death. The eastern sky glows a soft shade of lavender, then pink like stage lights on a canvas cyclorama. The night sky fades, so Orion, the Pleiades sisters, and Aquarius all retreat to their mythic lairs.

He jogs through the surf, heading south and back to Corn's busy wharf, but takes a long, slow approach. The final hem of night sky turns the color of fresh fruit, mango or banana. If he were home, he would call it peach. He considers the lands beyond his view: Colombia, Jamaica, and Cuba. This is as close as he will come this time, but he vows to return.

Rounding the southern point of the island, he watches work-boats heading out to sea. There are shrimpers, fishing boats with tall bridges, and open pangas making morning commutes. Each has a purpose, a quest, and a bounty to collect from the sea. He envies the goals that drive every Corn Island commuter and moves around the long curve of Brig Bay back to the wharf.

Today there is even more activity than he's seen before. Blinding light comes from an enormous Navy cutter dominating the principal dock. And men on the dock are armed with auto-matic weapons.

Inside the Promarblu commissary, he joins a line of hungry hands moving through the cafeteria line. The mood of the workers is elevated, even festive. He envies the way they grin at one another, trading jokes, sharing the morning. He tries to fit in but feels distant and separate.

Chance joins a crowded table and is welcomed with grunts. Each plate looks just the same: fried egg, tortillas, fried rice topped with beans. No one speaks. All eat with their heads down.

Back on the dock, the fully risen sun casts long, angular shadows on the only ship at the wharf. It is easily 100 feet long and brilliant white. Dark smoke drifts from a stack near the foredeck. Sturdy radio antennas rise above the bridge. An ornate crest resembling a coat of arms glows at the bow.

Men with aviator sunglasses stand motionless beside the ship. They wear green uniforms with pant legs tucked into spit-shined boots. Webbed belts sag beneath bellies from the weight of .45-caliber pistols and cartridge cases. Matching baseball caps bear their rank insignia. No man smiles as all watch the passing crowd.

Chance makes his way back to the dockmaster window. Inside, the tall man he met the day before sits in a transformed office. There are no boxes, no papers, and nothing to be seen on the floor. A large photographic portrait of *El Presidente* scowls on the back wall. Chance is sure the portrait was not there the day before. He leans into the crystal-clear window previously smudged with fingerprints.

"Morning," Chance calls out to the dockmaster.

"Ah, *Monsou* Chance. You are still here."

"Yes. Still here. But with your help, maybe not too much longer."

"Is it not beautiful today?" the dockmaster asks. "Is my island not the most beautiful in the world?"

"Yes, yes, quite beautiful. I have already been on a walk around the island today. I want to remember it well. I hope to bring friends from home here soon. But first... are any boats sailing to Bluefields today?"

"Today? It is Friday. No passenger boat on Friday."

"Yes, I know. Thought maybe you knew of someone heading out on their own. Someone I could speak to about a lift to Blue."

"Ah."

Again, the dockmaster shares strategies about hitching a ride to the mainland. He tells Chance to look for signs.

There will be no traffic at this dock as long as the "Big Ship" is here. He advises Chance to "respect" the men in the dark glasses and stand away from them. He suggests Chance hang around the "Little Dock," the smaller one past Rocky Point that typically services only Little Corn Island.

"Look for people with packages. People wearing jackets and coats. Women with shiny shoes. When the Big Cutter is here on the Island, all other traffic must stop. The people here all love *El Presidente*. And they love his family." Chance detects a tone of irony.

"Is that who's on the Big Cutter?"

"No. His son, and others, are expected today by plane."

"That explains the uniforms and all the pistols."

"I see no guns, my friend."

The dockmaster falls quiet. They look out at the cutter and the uniformed guards, bristling with weapons.

"The President may run Nic with a strong hand. But he does not own the people of Corn. Nor the wind. Nor the sea."

"So I should go to the Little Corn Island dock today? I have only ever seen it empty."

"Not today, my friend. Not with the Big Guy's family on the island. Watch the people. You will find what you seek. If not today, then perhaps the next. *Bonne chance*, Mr. Chance. *Bonne chance*."

The dockmaster leaves his post and heads straight for the Big Cutter, clipboard in hand. He greets the guards with a warm grin. Three men in uniform circle around him and examine many papers.

Chance merges into steady foot traffic on the shady side of the commercial wharf. He heads north on the *Vía Principal*, then veers west to Calle Promarblu and heads north for the smaller, usually empty dock serving Little Corn Island.

One cargo vessel is moored to the Little Corn dock. And today, dugouts, dinghies, and pangas are all tied up nearby. Chance has seen this dock before on previous island rambles, but never with this many boats. Two men sit on stumps in the shade, gazing intently at a small table between them. They play checkers.

A mid-morning breeze blows across the island from the west as Chance walks down the creaking dock. Waves slap against the side of the large boat tied up there. There is no sign anyone is on board, or, if anyone is, they are probably asleep. Chance measures the length of the vessel with his strides; it is about thirty meters. Reaching the stern and turning around, he learns that this is *Kathryn*, which has a home port in Puerto Limón. Standing on the dock for several minutes, he hears no movement onboard, so he heads back to the shore.

The two checker players halt their game and watch Chance approach. In size, physique, and wardrobe, they appear identical. They could easily be brothers, even twins. He gives them a wave, but they don't move.

"*Bonjou!*"

The two men nod and grunt in unison.

"That big boat there…" Chance shoots a thumb over his shoulder back at the dock. "That boat—the *Kathryn*—she's going to Little Corn?"

"Not today."

"Not today." One man speaks, and the other echoes.

"How 'bout tomorrow?" Chance suggests.

The two men turn, each looking at his mirror image as though the answer to this tricky question can be read in the eyes of his twin.

"Not tomorrow. Maybe never."

"Never? Then what's it doing here?" Chance wonders if the men are mocking him.

Through a long series of questions and duplicated answers, Chance learns the *Kathryn* sails soon for Panama. The two men are here to watch the ship and report if anyone goes on board. The captain is in town for the day. Only the captain knows when the ship will sail, and he is in town "visiting a good friend… yes, very good."

The captain will return before dark, and it might be possible to speak with him about the *Kathryn*'s departure, but they do not know if he will have time to speak. Chance thanks them and says he will return before sunset. The men pout their lips and watch the American leave before returning to their checker match. As he leaves the dockside, he is suddenly reminded of a silly endless children's rhyming game:

"Pete and Repeat were sitting on a fence. Pete fell off and who was left? Repeat!"

Chance feels he has met the twin muses from this childhood silliness, and now this idea won't leave his head.

Chance heads back inland through a patch of dense foliage filled with coconut, mango, and breadfruit. Buds of hibiscus are just popping out. The growing season here appears to be all year long. Back home in Virginia, there are probably still banks upon banks of wet snow.

Emerging from the brush, Chance hears the distinct drone of airplane engines throttling back for a landing at the *aeropuerto*, which lies just ahead on his way across the island. He concludes that it must be the LANICA flight arriving with the weekly "Friday Bank" to cash local checks.

He steps up his pace to watch the plane land. As soon as he hears the plane cut its engines, he hears another, and he watches a second plane land. Then a third one approaches. Three planes landing in this short a time, one behind the other, is very unusual at this quiet landing strip.

Chance stands near the terminal and sees three identical planes with official seals line up side by side. A squad of military men stand erect nearby. Squeaky yellow staircases are rolled to the rear of each plane. Clusters of men in dark suits seek shade beneath plane wings. The cargo holds and passenger doors are now open.

Women, men, and children in casual garb flow down the stairs. Then a stout man in a tropical shirt fills the cabin door of the plane nearest the terminal. He looks out across the airfield and gives a big wave. Cheers rise from the crowd hiding in the shade, which now spills onto the tarmac. The stout man grins broadly and descends the stairs.

There is much handshaking on the ground, then the new arrivals are ushered into a convoy of military vehicles. Motorcycles roar and the convoy departs in a tightly packed parade. Men in uniform quickly take defensive positions around the planes as workers offload the remaining suitcases and cargo.

Chance continues his trip back to the shack, but chooses the slightly longer scenic route, continuing on the *Vía Principal* past the *aeropuerto* and into the shady beating heart of the island.

He passes the sports ground, where there is a baseball diamond and a football field—not for what Chance calls football, but what he knows as soccer.

Families have already set blankets and chairs up for the weekend. Children kick soccer balls. A young crew marks foul lines on the baseball field with bright sand, which pops out against a sea of brilliant green. Chance makes a mental note to check out the action on Sunday when games are played from noon until midnight and sometimes later than that.

Just before the humble, single-story Seventh-day Adventist church, Chance turns onto the Calle La Loma, which leads back home through a tunnel of trees shading the road. He has already had a full day and hopes the shack is not too warm for a nap.

Chance knows he has arrived by the familiar "whop, whop, whop" sound of a machete on wood. He sees Master Carver and stops to watch. The old man speaks without looking up.

"*Bonjou*, Mistah Chance."

"*Bonjou*, Maestro Carver. You have a new work of art."

"You are too kind. It is what the Lord sends for me to do. I am lucky that every day he finds work for me. The day when there is none will be my last."

"That will be a long time from now."

The old carver looks up into the gringo's face. It is the first time Chance has seen his eyes. They are clouded and murky, as though they are floating in milk. The old man smiles, then grins, showing no teeth.

"I have already been here for a long time. Every day is a gift. From above. From the sea. I do not even know my age. Miss Nelly tells me it is more than one hundred. She tells me this every day for years. I know that I am one day old today because each day is the beginning of my life.

"And I know that my time is special here on Corn. It has taken all the history of the heavens to put me here. Every day is precious."

Chance, now seated, knees wrapped with his arms, watches the carver extract beauty from a twisted limb. He reflects on his college lessons. He thinks of ancient literature and suddenly sees Master Carver as an incidental but pivotal character from Shakespeare. Or something older, maybe from the Greeks. Something about wisdom and truth that is only seen through blind eyes. Maybe Oedipus. Maybe... Tiresias?

They sit quietly for several minutes. The gentle flapping of birds, splashing of distant surf, and shuffling of palms are abruptly interrupted by the thump of a coconut landing nearby.

"I believe you have not heard the news," says the carver.

"No. Probably not. I have not seen a newspaper in days. I don't remember when I last heard the radio."

"This is the important news. The news that affects us all. The news of Corn Island."

"Well, I know there are visitors on the island. There are more planes than usual. And there are boats."

"There is one who no longer needs a vessel of any kind."

"What do you mean?"

"He has taken the longest voyage and the shortest."

"Help me, Maestro Carver. I do not understand."

"Mistah Dean's son. Michael. He is gone."

"Back to Florida?"

"Back to the heavens. He is dead. Killed by a gun."

Chance needs time to let this news sink in. Can it be true? How would this man know?

"What? Mike Dean? I just saw him two days ago. Are you sure, Maestro?"

"As sure as the sun will set and the sea will rise and fall. As sure as these blind eyes can see."

"I must go," Chance says, stunned, not knowing what to say.

"I know, Mr. Chance. I know. You must go."

Dave lies propped on his bunk in the shack that they share. He is immersed in figures, which he jots on a work pad. His figures show a projected cash flow as the lobster fishing enterprise takes off, based on their recent successful one-day catch. It's much more satisfying projecting profits than calculating ongoing expenses. He figures that in one good year, barring drastic unforeseen disasters like a hurricane, the business could smoothly be working two boats with a monthly income of four to six hundred bucks. After that, the sky will be the limit.

Chance enters and collapses on his bed.

"Did you hear?"

"About Mike Dean? Yeah, I heard something. You?"

"Just heard from the carver man. What happened?"

"Don't know yet. Police came by. Wanted to talk to us. Told 'em what I knew."

"Which is...?"

"Not much. Haven't seen him for a day or two."

"Why'd they want to talk to us?"

"Well, maybe because we look like him? I don't know. Look... I got an errand to run. Gotta go back to Little Corn dock and speak to a guy. Fishin' Hole for dinner?"

"Yeah. Fine."

"See ya there."

Chance can't sit still. There's too much to process. Outside

Nelly's compound, it is tranquil. No kids are running around. Even the noisy birds have nothing to say.

He retraces tracks from earlier in the day, into the jungle and out. There are now more families on the sports field and vendors in the streets. The sun is going down, and the island is preparing for the weekend. He heads back to Little Corn dock.

There is quiet activity on the rarely used dock: two deck-hands flush and mop decks on a large vessel. A man pushes a cart up a ramp; another with a sea cap leans over the rail near the bridge.

Chance hails the man with the cap, who happens to be the captain. He asks about the ship's next stop. It will be Jamaica. When do they ship out? On Sunday. Could he hitch a ride? Impossible. The ship does not take passengers who are not pre-booked on international routes—rules of the company. The captain extends apologies that he can't help the stranded stranger.

"Sorry, Mon. Would like to help out, but can't be done."

"I understand. Any suggestions?"

"Catch a ride back to Rama, then Managua. You can get anywhere from there. Or take a plane. But I wouldn't. They're dangerous."

"So are the automatic weapons now on the island," thinks Chance. He thanks the captain, wishes him "fair winds and following seas," and receives a salute. He heads back to the wharf for a beer, hoping it will lift his mood.

However, the mood among regulars at the Fishin' Hole is glum. The reggae wailings from the jukebox seem particularly poignant. Chance sees Dek Jack the Jamaican with his regular company of young women in short skirts but takes a pint of beer to an empty table and sits down. Soon Dave joins him with his own pint. They greet with grunts and order dinner. The Seafood "Rundown" swimming in coconut milk tastes flat. They slurp mostly in silence.

"So, how'd your day go?" Chance finally asks.

"Spent the day working on figures. Jack helped with more traps. Took a swim. You?"

"Bit of a downer. Can't get over the thing with Mike Dean. What happened, do you think?"

"Killed himself."

"What? Killed himself? C'mon. No way—that kid was living the life."

"Had demons in his head. So, he tried to get rid of them. With a rifle. To the head."

"No..."

"Yep. Heard about it while I was with Trapper Man Jack. One of his buddies told him while I was there. Dropped what he was doing to go check it out. Paid a visit to the 'Grotto.' The police had apparently been there before. Cops wouldn't tell him anything. But folks outside knew it all. The boy did himself in. And it sounds very messy."

Once again, Chance is stunned. The hair on his neck grows erect.

"I just don't get it."

"Maybe he felt trapped. Not living his life," Dave speculates.

"What more could anyone want than this?"

Dave gives his partner a familiar, knowing look. They sit silently, eating, for several minutes.

"Spoke with the skipper of a big boat. It's heading to Jamaica on Sunday."

"Did you get a ride?"

"Naw. Skipper said he couldn't do it. Something about international waters. I thought they were all international."

"He was probably talking about passports."

"Well, I've got one. Right here." Chance pats the pouch beneath his shirt.

"That's a Yankee passport."

"Damn right it is. We can go anywhere."

"But you still gotta go through customs and Border Patrol unless you're a pirate. Remember getting down here?"

"Well, what about you when you're ready to go back? Aren't you going soon?"

"Yeah. But my passport is Jamaican."

The crowd in the Fishin' Hole builds. Two young women sitting at a table nearby seem to be watching Dave and Chance.

"I'm heading back to Nelly's. You ready to go?"

"Not right yet. Seems I've got an appointment." Dave salutes the table of two ladies with a raised glass.

"Oh. I see. Guess I'll meet you back at the shack."

"Mmm. Maybe. Don't wait up."

PAYING
RESPECTS

News of Mike Dean's death sweeps across Corn Island like a tropical storm. The information creates gusts of speculation about what really happened.

There are many versions of the cause and details. News of any event of island-wide interest travels by way of "coconut telegraph." It travels fast, person to person. But like the childhood game "telephone," stories change from person to person. Facts in a story told across the island or even across the room are only as reliable as one's confidence in the last speaker.

One story calls it a domestic incident, following a confrontation within the family. Another explanation cites use of drugs since it is well known these gringos have a liberal attitude toward pot and hallucinogens, maybe even LSD. The head of the family, Don Dean, frequently travels back to the mainland, going as far as Panama and even Colombia. No telling what he brings back. Or the death of young Dean could have come from a dare, perhaps a drinking challenge gone wrong. Some speculate that an intruder killed Mike. But no one knows for sure.

One thing is for sure. There is no real police force on Big Corn. No hospital. No doctors. Families take care of themselves. Locals rely on traditional remedies for mental, spiritual, and physical cures. Diagnoses from elders are the most respected. Their directions are followed closely because they have seen the most births, illnesses, and accidents. Priests and chaplains are called upon day and night to confirm deaths.

Fish packers from the Promarblu processing co-op often end up as de facto coroners. There is no hospital, no clinic, no doctor's office, no clinical emergency care. Medicines, salves, and balms for common complaints like stomachaches, sinus problems, headaches, colds, and insect bites are found at the Chinese store, with diagnoses and treatments prescribed by whoever is behind the counter.

In this uncertain environment, only one thing seems sure. All the stories agree that young Mike Dean is dead.

Dave has been out all night, but he returns to the shack midmorning. He finds Chance on his bunk, reading, and is surprised because they are usually both somewhere near the water at this time of day. Their previous road buddy status has been on hiatus since Chance's announcement of departure.

"Hey. Surprised to see you here."

"Just catching up on some details. Thought it was a good time to count my fortune. Big night on the town?"

"Well… you know… received an offer I couldn't refuse."

"Just one?"

"Watch it, mate. Miss Pansy's a nice girl."

"OK. OK. I'm sure she is. How 'bout her mom?"

"Can you stop it?"

"Sorry."

Chance goes back to his reading. Dave digs through a pile of clothes, pulls out his wrinkled wardrobe for the day, and does a quick hand press of the shorts and shirt on his bed. He dashes out for a shower. Chance gets up, slings on his document pouch, and covers it up with a favorite faded shirt. He puts a few items in his pockets, slides into laceless sneakers, and decides which of three different routes to take to return to Little Corn dock to check on departing boats there and then move on to the "Grotto" to pay respects. It's nearly as warm in the shack as it is outside. Time to go… anywhere.

Dave crashes back in, smelling like soap, with one hand holding a towel around his waist.

"You off?"

"Yeah. Thought I'd go look in on Don Dean. Offer condolences."

"Get ready for a crowd."

"Really? Lotta people?"

"How about the whole island? Dean is a big name around here."

"Big as 'Stasio… little Presidente?"

"Almost. At least today. Hey… I ran into Jack. He's got more traps for us. He's also got the scoop on what really happened to Mike Dean. Suicide, he says."

Trapper Jack has become their most credible source for island information. They've seen him in action on the sand and in the bars. In addition, Dave is a customer. Dave tells Chance that Jack heard the same story they have, but from a different grapevine. Jack wanted to know the truth, so he went to the scene of the incident, the Deans' home, to "…see for meself."

When Trapper Jack arrived at the "Grotto," Don Dean was not in the yard as he usually was, working on motors and boats. But many islanders were there, whispering in groups. Jack lumbered toward the house, nodded at familiar faces, and stepped up to the door. Jenny met him there.

"I've come to see the young man."

"Mike is not here. Well, he is, but he isn't."

"Yes, ma'am. And Mr. Dean. Mr. Dean is here?"

"He's here. But he's not able to see anyone right now."

Jack knew that time was short. Dead bodies on the island stay above ground for only a few hours, just long enough to make sure there is no mistake. That is why everyone on Corn Island knows from a young age exactly where their body will lie until the end of time.

"Yes. I see. The young man. Can I tell him goodbye?"

"If that's what you want. He's there. Under the sheet."

She pointed to a shrouded form lying on the floor at the edge of the porch and retreated into darkness inside. The boards groaned as Jack walked over to it. He took a knee and gently pulled back the sheet. He saw two pale gray feet in open-toe sandals and quickly covered them back up. He moved to the opposite end of the form and again pulled back the sheet. There, he saw a face much closer to the floor than he expected. Lips parted, eyelids half drawn over still eyes. The face looked more like an effigy carved from marble than the maturing man Jack had often seen walking through town or launching a boat out to sea.

The brawny Jamaican examined the face he no longer knew. There was an opening just above one ear near the temple congealed with blood—the bullet's entry wound. The face lay nearly flat against a folded towel stained completely dark red with blood. There was no back to the head.

"Rest well, my young friend. Rest well. You are already home."

Jack replaced the sheet and rose slowly. He kept his chin tight to his chest, clasped his hands, and said a quiet prayer. Then he turned, stepped off the porch, spoke to no one, and left.

The trapper made his way back to his work shed. Small waves broke on the shore like a muffled drumroll. Unseen grackles saluted the big man as he returned. He found Dave sitting on the sand, grimacing as he struggled to weave another trap with uncooperative sticks and reluctant wire. The two

Jamaicans sat side by side, one the color of night, the other pale as unprinted newspaper stock. Jack spoke first.

"It is true what they say."

"Yes?"

"The young man is gone. Mr. Mike Dean is dead. I see him and know for sure."

"You have been to the 'Grotto'?"

"All of the island will go there today and then to the grave-yard. It is how we keep the dark angels away. And it is how we show respect."

"Should I go to see the family? Or wait for the burial?

"That is for you to say, Mon. The young man killed himself. This is disrespect to the spirits. It is a weakness in the heart and the head."

Now, back at the shack, Dave recounts the story to Chance as it was told to him by Jack. Looking in a small mirror while he speaks, he puts the final twist on a brightly colored ascot that Chance has not seen before.

"At least, that's what Big Jack told me. No reason to doubt him. Saw it all with his own eyes."

"Pretty fuckin' chilling. Like something from a movie."

"It's life. Well, maybe, death... guess it's where they get the stories for movies. You know... fact is stranger than fiction and all that."

"Not the kind of movie I want to see."

"I'm out. See you later." Dave departs.

Soon, Chance is out on the road as well. The day is hot and humid. The sun has been up for hours. Without stopping at the co-op, Chance buys a few packs of wrapped "biscuits" that he calls "cookies" at the Chinese store and gulps down a soft drink, calling it breakfast. He heads slowly through the shade back to Little Corn dock.

The cargo ship *Kathryn* sits quietly, waiting for departure. Now there's another much smaller vessel, about thirty-six feet stem to stern, tied behind her. It is a wooden craft with a small bridge at the forecastle and a tarp-covered deck. Chance walks up and down the dock and sees *"Nereida"* painted on her stern.

Chance watches two young men load sacks of rice into the forward hold. Their taut, tight torsos gleam in the sun as they move from dock to deck and back. He greets them with "Hola"s and inquires, *"Habla inglés?"*

Both shake their heads but point to a short, ruddy man walking toward them on the dock. They exchange "Hola"s and then "Hello"s.

"You speak English?"

"A little," the seaman responds, making the pinched thumb and finger gesture Chance knows well by now.

"Are you skipper of this boat?"

"I am skipper. Is my boat," he says, patting the prow as proof. "You call me Cap."

"Bueno, bueno. That's good news. Do you sail to the Main? Back to Bluefields?"

"Yes. Back to Bluefields. Tomorrow."

"Do you take passengers? Can a man ride on your boat?"

"This boat takes many passengers. Do you wish to ride?"

"Yes. To Bluefields. If you have the room."

"Yes. Yes. We have the room for you. There will be others, too."

They strike a deal. The *Nereida* departs the day after tomorrow "with the rising tide" at 7 p.m. The gringo is welcome to ride back to Blue at that time. The fare is thirty córdobas, about $2. Skipper "Cap" prefers to be paid just before they leave. He explains that, that way, he is sure to carry the cords home to

Bluefields, "and not leave them here on Corn." Chance is pleased with the terms and agrees to meet in the same place the next day, well before dark. They part with a handshake. Cap climbs back on board and rattles commands to his two young hands. Chance walks quickly down the dock as though a heavy load has been lifted from his back. But there is a lot to do and not much time.

Chance heads north on the island toward the "Grotto." He takes a jungle path to stay in the shade and makes good headway. En route, he stops at two different stores and buys a few provisions —more biscuits and tins of canned fish—and adds them to his pouch. It seems odd to buy packaged items here in this Eden of fresh fruit, surrounded by an ocean of seafood. But these provisions will be eaten tomorrow and the next day, if necessary, aboard *Nereida*.

Chance has learned to take nothing for granted in this country. In his head, he suddenly hears the voice of a deceased grandfather who often laughed and said, "Leave nothing to Chance." He finally understands the irony in these words.

He enters the grounds of the "Grotto," the sheltered home on a small hill hidden by a cove but with a clear, elevated view of the sparkling Caribbean. People are scattered beneath the trees and out on the beach. Men gather in the area where boats are upturned and engines are mounted on what Chance knows as "sawhorses," but which people here call "seahorses."

Strange faces mill around, admiring Don Dean's outdoor shop and its beneficial arrangement of hand tools on sheltered pegboards. Chance sees Henri's family of brothers squatting together on the sand near the high-water mark. They give him discreet waves. Everyone seems to be waiting.

Chance walks up the rise toward the house. Miss Nelly whispers to a group and nods as Chance passes by. He must tell her about his imminent departure, but not now.

People on the path step back to allow the gringo to pass. The near absence of voices among so many people seems eerie. He neither sees nor hears any children. At the top of the hill, Jenny stands behind the screen of the front door.

"Hello, Miss Jenny."

"Chance," she steps out on the porch.

"Is Dean here? I've come to say hello."

"He's not seeing anyone just now."

"I understand. Is there anything I can do for him? For you?"

"Just look around. I have all the help I need. More than enough."

"Nothing? Anything?"

"We could use a doctor. For Dean, not the boy. The fish packers will be here soon to take care of Mike." Tears well in her eyes. She has been crying for some time. "We need everything. We need someone in charge. This is no way to live. No way to die." She looks at the shrouded corpse. Then she turns and goes inside.

Chance goes over to the sheet-covered body. He looks out through the palms, smells the sea, and tries to remember how one might stand at a solemn, Christian moment. He straightens, looks above the trees for guidance, but finds none, then looks down. He has no urge to pull back the cloth. Dave's description is vivid enough.

"Why did you do this? What were you thinking? You have everything… everything here."

He stands for several moments over the covered body of Mike Dean, who was only a few years younger than him. He thinks about his plans to leave Corn Island but wonders how Mike's way out could be a choice. He stands silent and alone for several minutes.

Moving back down the hill, Chance stops at the clutch of

females gathered with Miss Nelly. The ladies fall silent and stand back. Nelly and Chance stand face-to-face.

"Did you hear how it happened?" Nelly asks.

"Yes. Dave spoke with Trapper Jack."

"Sad. Very sad," says Nelly.

"Miss Jenny says Don Dean needs a doctor. Should I get a doctor? Where will I find him?"

"It will take a long time. Perhaps a day. There is no doctor on the island. A doctor must come from Bluefields... or beyond."

"No doctor on Corn Island? There are hundreds of people living here—maybe two or three thousand. How can this many people live without a doctor? There are babies born every week."

"And... many die."

"But surely there are trained emergency professionals. Firemen. Nurses."

"Only those in the families. The families practice the medicine."

"What about the police? They must be trained in first aid. Life support."

"Do you see the police? The firemen? We have none. There are no funds for these things here on Corn."

The ladies nod in rhythm to Nelly's words. They move gently as one, like the choir behind a preacher. Nelly stretches her hands toward Chance. They are deeply creased, and he recognizes calluses at their joints. She sees he is stunned.

"Do you see these hands, Mr. Chance? These hands. All of these hands...?" She spreads her arms wide as though in a pulpit, indicating the choir swaying around her. "These are the doctors. The nurses. The firefighters. The ones gathering those coming into this world. These are the hands that will send us all home. It is the way of the island. It is the way of our world here on Corn."

Chance takes in Nelly's words but saves them for interpretation at another time. He absorbs the spectacle of familiar faces from across the island gathered here at the "Grotto" in silent clumps beneath the trees.

There are fishermen, lobstermen, and dockhands he has seen every morning at the Promarblu Co-op. The clerk from the Chinese store, patrons from the Fishin' Hole, servers from Hotel Playa Coca—they are all living here in this twisted paradise without the security or support he has taken for granted in the States. This place is wilder than he ever imagined, a raw, primitive place—an area that is ripe for domination by a selfish autocrat and perhaps a revolution.

He sees a group of men dressed in clerical robes in a tight circle separate from the others, their heads leaning in together. These must be the men from all the churches on the island: Catholic, Anglican, Jehovah's Witness, Seventh-day Adventist. Standing just behind them in another concentric circle are young men in choir robes, shorts, and sandals, also with their heads bowed. They listen to the softly spoken words of a tall man with bright white hair, holding a large book in both hands.

At the bottom of the hill, Chance sees a cluster of island visitors. He recognizes Jeffrey and John, the two medical research students living briefly at Mount Pleasant. They begin the climb toward the house with two other young men dressed nearly identically to them. Chance meets them on their way up.

"Hey, guys."

"Chance! You're here. We got a notice on the shortwave," says Jeffrey or John.

"Said we could be of some help here. What's going on?" asks the other J.

"Well... the young man who lives here—used to live here—apparently pulled a trigger on himself. He's dead. Body's on the porch."

"You're sure he's dead? No pulse?"

"Didn't check his pulse. But there's no head. Blasted his own skull off with a rifle. He's dead."

The four medical students look at each other, wide-eyed. They do not comment. Chance explains that Mike Dean's father, Don, and Don's partner, Jenny, are in the house. He tells the med students that Dean might need some professional help. But there's no doctor on the island.

"Not sure what's going on with the father, but apparently, he is in the wrong way. Maybe you can help."

"You know we're not doctors, right?"

"At least not yet," chimes the other J.

"Yeah. I know. But you're more doctors than I am. The closest real doc right now is half a day away at Bluefields. Maybe you could just go talk to them. They could use a little help."

Chance watches the aspiring MDs move quickly up the path to the house. The soft voices of bystanders on the hill blend with the syncopated thrum of low tide surf. The sun is now sinking over the sea.

Retracing his steps on the *Vía Principal*, Chance hears the sounds of Saturday night. He has heard that there will be an open-air screening of a film on the sports field. People dressed in brighter colors than the mourners head that way. What he is seeing now could be any other place he's been in the world.

People go by, bright-eyed and fast-talking with the prospect of something out of the ordinary about to happen. Men collect on benches like flies. They laugh and pick at their feet, trying to conceal what they are watching, the passage of this one pale fellow walking alone down the street.

Passing bars, Chance hears country and western music mixed with reggae on jukeboxes. He hears the bellowing of working men who have found the elusive answers to vexing questions of the universe at the bottom of the last pitcher of cerveza. They must be declared right now and shared with those who are barely listening. Chance recognizes that this Saturday night's excitement is not so different to what he left behind in the mountains of Virginia.

A glint of gold from a girlish grin is enough to turn the heads of a group of swains with slicked hair on motorbikes. They will engage in all-night games of cat and mouse with no real expectation of consummation. The scene reminds him of his own lustful wandering on Saturday nights.

Then, with no warning, Chance hears the rumble of several slow-moving vehicles and sees his shadow outlined on the sandy road by a harsh blinking of lights coming from behind. It is a rapidly approaching motorcade. Pedestrians move quickly aside as three armored vehicles pass by. They are the same ones he saw earlier at the airport.

Chance wants no part of whatever will happen next. He veers off into the jungle, where the darkness is stacked against him. His eyes adjust as he makes his way down a narrow path to Nelly's shack.

Chance spends the rest of his night alone, packing. He thinks about his life on the brink of the future, and wonders where he will meet his life partner. He is not looking at this time for a casual coupling, like Dave and Pansy, but a real, dedicated partner, someone to spend a lifetime with.

He compares all the opportunities before him with the abrupt end of life of a maturing man only three or four years younger than himself. What could drive someone to take their own life as they stand on the brink of adulthood? And he wonders if this is an omen.

For the time being, Chance is alone and prefers it this way. He puts down the book he's reading and opens his journal to make notes about the day. His streams of thought are turbulent and disjointed. He can make no sense of them. He extinguishes the candle and drops almost instantly into deep sleep.

DAY OF REFLECTION

Again, Chance wakes before dawn, something he rarely does at home. He hears no snoring from the other bed and lights a candle. He is alone. No Dave for the third night in a row. His partnership with Pansy must be going well.

Waning moonlight cuts through the trees at a sharp angle as Chance takes a "bucket shower." Shivering in the shack and covered in goose pimples, he takes stock of what he needs to leave the island. Then he makes a pile of things to leave behind, mostly paperback books.

Chance heads for breakfast at the commissary. It opens early even on a Sunday, and he hopes to be first in line, but he's not. He asks for extra helpings of rice and beans from servers he does not recognize. They shrug and do as he asks at no extra charge.

In minutes, he's back on the street, where *El Presidente*'s military cutter still dominates the dock. Uniformed guards on deck and at the ramp watch him pass by. He wonders what they can see through their dark glasses before the sun comes up.

Just beyond the dock, a man with tousled gray hair, a twisted open shirt, stained work pants, and bare feet moans at the base of a palm. Squinting through one eye, he shouts out, "I'm a rummin' son of a bitch," then bays like a banshee before curling up for a nap. He is a remnant of Saturday night and a reminder of how, for some hourly workers, Sunday is not that much different from the days before.

Back at Nelly's, Chance washes clothes in a pail and hangs them on a line to dry. Then he sits in the room's one chair at the rickety table to catch up on his journal. He plays back events in his head from the past few days. The images flicker in his memory like trailers at the movie house.

Suddenly, panic grips him.

What if *Nereida* has already left, without him? He is confident he was told it was scheduled to depart on Monday, and from the chiming bells he now begins to hear, he is certain the day is Sunday. However, he also knows events on the island unfold at their own pace. He's seen no calendars except the one he marks in his daybook. The only reliable timepiece here is the tide. He races out the door.

Little Corn dock is less than a mile from the shack. Chance runs the whole way. Pacing his breathing to his footfalls, he notices how much easier it is to run now than it was before he and Dave started this trip. The challenges, physical effort, and sharpening senses have all made him more fit and alert. Also, he is keen to see *Nereida* still at the dock.

He does not slow down until his foot falls with a thud on the wooden dock. He stops and catches his breath. *Nereida* sits proudly alone, bobbing in the rising tide, tiny waves slapping against her side. Chance is hugely relieved. He scolds himself for his doubt, then gently chuckles. "Typical," he says, recognizing a tendency to court failure, disappointment, and even tragedy in his brain even when there is none.

Walking all the way to the end of the dock, he examines the

full length of the boat, stops at the stern, and looks out to sea. The sun scales the backside of a flotilla of giant clouds sailing toward South America. Church bells chime in the distance. He thanks the Lord for this moment. He confirms in his mind, against still another brilliant backdrop, that leaving Corn Island now is the right thing to do

Back on the sandy road, families move in groups. He sees Nelly with several children coming toward him, all dressed for church. He recognizes the boys who play outside his shack and the three girls Nelly has introduced to him and Dave. The eldest daughter, who is walking directly beside Nelly, is shapely, shy, and looks to be about eighteen, but he was proudly told on the day they met that she was "just fourteen." At the time, Chance wondered if the introduction was the opening move in some transaction. Fruit grows lush in the tropics and ripens early.

"Good morning, Miss Nelly."

"Good morning, Mistah Chance. And may God bless you on this Sunday. We are on our way to being with the Anglicans. Maybe you will join us." Nelly speaks in her soft, modulating singsong voice, almost a choir unto herself.

Four boys, dressed for church in bright white shirts, seize the moment to chase one another in the street. The three sisters group tightly around their mother—the oldest stares intently at her shiny shoes.

"Thank you so much. Not today. I have already had my moment with the Lord."

"Ah, so."

"He has given us a beautiful day today."

"Indeed. They are all beautiful, and abundant, in their way."

Chimes ring out. They listen together as they toll. He counts eight.

"Can you tell me how everything went yesterday? Do you have a moment?"

"For you, Mistah, I have all the time."

179

Nelly calls to her boys and has them gather by her. Nelly, seven children, and Chance congregate beneath a cluster of palms, stirring shadows on the sand. Nelly tells Chance how the medical students met with Don Dean and gave him comfort. She describes how a contingent of strong men from the fish processing plant arrived with a large bag and took "Mistah Mike" to the cemetery for a private ceremony. Nelly was privileged to be part of the group. Stewards from the island churches placed the corpse in the grave. Pastors from every congregation blessed Mike Dean's new home. Women of the churches set out a meal for all to share.

"It sounds quite peaceful."

"This is our way."

"And Mr. Dean?"

"Miss Jenny was with him. And the Lord."

Church chimes ring out again—this time too many to count.

"We must go."

"I know. Me too."

"I know."

"Oh… no, not to the church. I am leaving the island soon. Tomorrow, with the tide."

"I know. We must go now." Nelly steps forward, as do all the children, toward one particular chiming bell.

Chance is not surprised that Nelly knows his plans. He heads back to the compound as the heat clicks up a notch, despite a robust onshore breeze.

"You want a hand today with some traps?" Chance asks back at the shack.

"No thanks, mate. I'm all set. Jack is just wrapping up the final one of the six. Henri and I will drop them tomorrow. Probably about the same time that you're heading out."

Dave cannot resist this easy dig. Chance's bristly conscience scolds him. He feels guilty leaving Dave to make it all on his own, though this was always the plan. Still, Chance feels as though he's bailing on his friend.

Dave is sensitive about Chance's departure. In truth, since arriving on the island, every topic has gotten touchy, particularly when it comes to cash. But Chance is ready to settle up as best they can.

"I still owe you some money for the car. After all, you and Myrtle got me here to Nica."

"Well. If you can afford it."

"I can sign over some traveler's checks. I think I still owe you about a hundred."

"Yeah. 'Bout that. If you can afford it, I won't say no."

Chance endorses AmEx checks and hands them to Dave. The $100 is a sizable chunk of his ready cash stash, but, with a little luck, he will be able to replenish it in Managua. He has learned how to live frugally, and, back on the mainland, they take credit cards. Rental payments from tenants at his fixer-upper home back in the States pay the bills his credit card accrues. He uses the card as a backup, which hasn't been possible on the island. It is challenging to get folks to take even traveler's checks here.

Chance is eager to conclude this transaction. "Wanna get out and see some sights? I'm going over to the ballpark. They say Sunday is always the big day."

"Think I'll stay here," says Dave. "I've got some figuring to do. The past week's been busy. Next week will be even busier... 'specially by myself."

"Pansy'll be here."

"Pansy? Leave her out of this. We're friends. That's all. She's got her own work to do. How many women have you seen out on the water?"

Once again, Chance hits a raw nerve. Maybe he means to, maybe not. It's the kind of banter that passes quickly at fraternity houses back at college. However, those days are far behind and thousands of miles away.

"OK. Sorry, sorry. Didn't mean it as an insult. Let's just keep it light."

"What do you know about Pansy?"

"Word gets around. Nothing bad. We're living on an island. Stories have nowhere to go. Just 'round and 'round, until the next one breaks."

"Don't hear much about you out there."

"I'm boring. And there's been a lot of other news."

Stepping out of the doorway into the midday heat, the gringo shades his eyes and looks back at his Jamaican friend.

"See you at the ball field."

"Probably not. Unless they're playing cricket."

"Not bloody likely, mate," says Chance affecting a soft British accent.

"I'll pass on the game. Don't really understand how it's played. Dinner tonight? Something nice. Might be our last." New dollars in Dave's pocket seem to brighten his disposition. Maybe his funding is tighter than Chance thought.

"Fishin' Hole? About dark?"

"Sounds good. Cheers, then."

"Cheers."

Chance walks across the compound. Again, he hears the tolling of bells, this time coming from every direction. Services have ended. Through the trees, he sees people heading home. Tantalizing cooking fragrances fill the yard.

Master Carver sits on a bench at his small hut. He wears a fresh pastel shirt, a woven straw hat with a narrow brim, and sunglasses. Smooth, shining wooden handles lie at his feet. He appears to be waiting for customers interested in his hand-hewn wares.

"Good morning, Master."

"Good morning, Mistah Chance."

"You look to be waiting for guests, for company."

"Everyone will be on the path today. And this is the best place to be."

"I see. I wish you well."

"To you the same, my friend."

Many people go by on the road, smiling and nodding as they pass. On the *Vía Principal*, Chance joins a stream heading for the center of the island. They seem to all have the same end in mind.

The Estadio Municipal de Béisbol is painted in the vivid colors of the Nicaraguan flag. It pops like an eye chart against its surroundings. Chance joins a crowd of fans pushing inside. Tickets are cheap, and so is the beer. There are no seats in the stadium, just alternating striped blue-and-white platforms. Chance finds a spot along the first-base foul line, which grows more and more crowded as the day wears on. Fortunately, this is the "shady" side.

Teams warm up on the well-worn field. Two announcers on the public address microphone speak nonstop in Spanish and Creole with intermittent snatches of English. They welcome the crowd over and over and provoke them to purchase cerveza and chicharrones. There is frequent praise for *El Presidente*.

Finally, the opening ceremonies get underway. Every player, coach, assistant, water boy, and grounds attendant is introduced, then they run out on the field and take their place along the foul lines. Two agitated schoolteachers guide a column of children in uniform to the pitcher's mound. They finally sing the national anthem together, but their voices are drowned out by the accompanying time-delayed loudspeaker audio. The singers receive raucous applause and cheers from the crowd anyway. This is followed by a long, winding introduction of a local celebrity. A medal is pinned to his chest, and, with great fanfare, he throws out the first ball, which almost makes it to home plate.

The game begins. Chance watches every pitch almost as intently as he examines the crowd. There are disputed calls causing slamming of bats against the ground. A homer or two. Many close plays at every base require official intervention. One player is dismissed from the game, and then another.

There is significant interruption of play in the fourth inning brought on by a clear and unmistakable "ground-rule double." One manager and then the other race to discuss the ruling with the umpire at the plate. Major discord. Players rush to the infield. Others clear benches and confront each other near third base, then also at first. There is friction in the outfield, where pitchers leave their bullpens to share boisterous opinions with the opposition.

The crowd boos. Another contingent cheers. The boo-ers crank up again, louder, and so do the opposing fans. Spectators push and shove one another. Then, as if by magic, it's over. Managers leave the field.

Another batter comes to the box—the crowd cheers. The game resumes, and a climax occurs in the seventh inning. A huge mama pig bloated with piglets finds her way to the park and makes agonizing progress across the infield. Play is halted. No one moves to remove the pig, as she seems to be on a critical maternal mission. Fans begin to clap. Their applause grows rhythmic.

Female voices begin cheering and are supported by melodic wailing. The sow is unfazed in her journey from third base to first. As she leaves through a gate opened by a parking attendant, she receives cheers and an ovation greater than any other throughout the day.

Chance watches the entire game, won by the home team 7 to 4. However, the heat from the direct sun and a sweaty, ever-growing crowd encourage him to leave. It's been fun to watch, but now it's time to go. He heads to Morgan's Hotel.

Like nearly every enterprise on the island, Morgan's Hotel is run by one family, the Hookers. Chance is pleased and surprised to learn he shares the same family name as the owners.

Gentle Mr. Hooker apparently handles the front desk twenty-four hours a day. When not greeting guests, checking them in, or directing recent arrivals to local attractions, he reads sports magazines in the most comfortable chair in the lobby. Mrs. Hooker, Eloise (pronounced "El-oyse"), controls the kitchen, the dining room, and the cleaning staff. These duties are mostly accomplished. The staff is mostly is mostly up of the Hooker children, some with spouses from across the island. "Miss Fern" is descended from another important island family, the Downs.

Like Hatfields and McCoys, there is a long, legendary history of dispute and accommodation between these families. Controversies still arise, and lines are often drawn in the sand depending on one's grandparents' name. However, for the most part, economic necessity has drawn the two powerful families together. Two family legacies through the resulting offspring are better than one.

Chance asks where the hotel's namesakes, the Morgans, are.

"Ah, Captain Morgan was the greatest pirate of the Caribbean. But we are not pirates."

"I have heard of the captain. Why choose his name for your hotel?"

"People come to the island for the sea. They come for adventure."

"And to relax."

"Yes, to relax. We have the finest beds on the island. Some say also the finest dining room."

"But your name is Hooker."

"This is true."

"Why not call your hotel Hooker's?"

"Too much history. Too much family."

"I would like to learn the history of the island. Do you have a book?"

"The book is still being written. By my cousin Miss Alva. She can tell you it all. She lives on the island's north end near the cemetery. She always welcomes guests. You must visit with her."

"I would like that, but I'm not sure I have time."

"Perhaps another visit. Here's her address anyway."

"Thanks."

Chance is packed and ready to go. He walks down to Little Corn dock, where *Nereida* is set to cast off. He speaks with a deckhand and confirms the vessel is ready to depart but will not leave before the "main tide" tomorrow. He explains he is joining the crew on its trip back to the mainland, and the unfamiliar sailor allows him to stow his bag on board. However, for now, Chance has time on his hands.

He takes the jungle route north toward the Baptist church and nearby island cemetery. As he passes the graveyard, through a crooked garden of memorial stones, he notices the raw dirt of a new grave at the far edge of the yard. It must be Mike Dean's. He says a silent prayer and moves on.

Arriving at the island's northern shore, he turns east and

soon comes to a neat clutch of cabins on the point. Following the directions provided by Mr. Hooker at Morgan's Hotel desk, he finds a cabin with a carved plaque that reads "Alva Hooker, North End." He knocks at the door, and soon it opens.

"Miss Alva?"

"Yes."

"My name is Chance. Your cousin Mr. Hooker at Morgan's said you might have time for a word with me. I am interested in your study of the history of the island."

Alva is a slender woman of about sixty with quick, darting eyes. She invites Chance inside and guides him to one of two sturdy rocking chairs with armrests worn smooth by years of use. The chairs dominate a well-appointed room with a large picture window providing a clear view of the channel separating Big and Little Corn Islands. She offers tea. Chance thanks her and asks for lemon only.

Family pictures hang all around, and a bookcase fills one entire wall. Papers are precisely piled on the floor. Books lie open on tables. Though the room is crowded, there is a fastidious order to the clutter. Miss Alva returns and sets down a delicate tea set on the window seat before the rockers. She dives right in, like a college professor at the lectern.

"The history of the islands is really the history of two families. Others come and go. But Hookers and Downs have made the Islands of Corn."

"These are two islands with the same name. They are like family but more distant cousins than brothers or sisters."

Miss Alva pauses to explain that she is a schoolteacher. They are between terms, so she is happy to sit with Chance. The school will begin soon, in a few weeks, near the end of the month (February), so her time is now her own, and she is pleased to share it with a "new friend from the United States." She has made a life of studying families, and she feels lucky not to have children of her own.

"At the school, I am one teacher who can be fair and balanced. I do not confuse loyalty the way so many mothers and fathers in families do. There is always the favorite son or most reliable daughter. They get the most attention. There is the same in schools if one allows it. I treat all of my students equally. Fairly, they all agree."

Chance sits silently but restlessly, with all the patience of a twenty-five-year-old with a big boat trip coming up. He examines Miss Alva's face as she looks out to the channel separating Big Corn and Little Corn Islands. Her eyes squint above sharp cheekbones as though reading sheet music from a distance, cautious not to miss any beat in this familiar song.

"There are many stories about the islands, as you might imagine. Even about the name, which comes from the days of pirates. Have you noticed a great deal of corn growing on the island?"

Chance shakes his head. She looks again to sea, removing an embroidered handkerchief from one sleeve and placing it in her lap as though it were a weapon or a shield.

"The islands have been known as 'Corn' since the days of the buccaneers. The name you hear now and see on maps, 'Isla Grande del Maize,' came much later. Even then, centuries ago, it is not clear that there was ever any corn.

"Some say that corn in bags, the way we transport rice today, was once used as currency. The locals that pirates and traders found here were good with their hands, both on the land and at sea. Indians learned to cultivate crops to serve with fish, shrimp, and lobster here. So, some say, the islands became the Islands of Corn, Big and Little. But that seems unlikely. There are so few seeds of corn found on the ground today."

"Maybe they washed out to sea," Chance suggests.

"Maybe. Or maybe they left with the Indians who used the ears and kernels as money. But there is another theory." Miss Alva takes a slow slurp from her cup.

"The Corns were popular with the corsairs who sailed the Caribbean, en route to Cuba, Dominica, Antilles, even Cartagena. There are many ports across the Caribbean and always ships with many hungry sailors.

"Another story has it our islands were breeding grounds. For cattle, swine, all sorts of livestock. No doubt you see remnants of stone walls in the jungle. The rocks were hauled down from Mount Pleasant, then stacked near the sites of large homes. These were ranches, for cattle. But they often called cattle by the Spanish word '*carne*.' Do you speak Spanish, Mr. Hooker?"

"Very little."

"*Carne* means 'meat.' The story goes that the islands were known for *carne*, which was bought, traded, and often stolen by hungry men from the sea. Our islands became the *Carne* Islands, and, with time, the name changed, by tongue, not the written word, as English-speaking seamen called it 'Corn.' And so now the islands became the Corn Islands."

"Interesting. Makes sense."

Chance is quite sure Dave will have a firm opinion on the etymology of the Corn Islands.

"Of course, these are stories. There is no hard evidence. It is what one chooses to believe. There is another story.

"During the day of the corsairs, it is said there was a time when *carne*, that meat on the shores of the island, was human. Men shoved overboard during battles at sea, pirate raids, and mutinies swam or washed up here. They died on shore, some perhaps waiting for a rescue that never came. The beaches became littered with corpses, then skeletons."

Chance winces at this image. He cannot help but think of Mike Dean and his quiet resting place nearby.

"And when pirates hid treasure here, not just on Mount Pleasant, but all about the island, they used skeletons as warnings. They built fences with crosses on which they hoisted dead bodies, so they would be seen by ships at sea. For many years, ships refused to come to the Corns, which were said to be 'haunted.'

"Now. There are times—mainly during the season of rain—when islanders hear the moaning of the dead. The dead from long ago. And, each year, during the first days of November, we listen for these sounds.

"Children dress like ghouls and phantoms. We gather on the shore, some sleeping there, and howl into the wind to keep evil spirits of Death far away at sea. At the same time, we honor those who have gone before, our ancestors who we all will follow."

Miss Alva pauses. She stares hard across the channel, as if caught in a moment from years ago. Chance remains quiet. He has been discreetly making notes in his journal.

"These are legends and traditions. But I am a scholar, a person who believes in facts. These facts I know…"

Miss Alva launches into confirmation of stories Chance has now pieced together from other sources while on the island. She speaks of the fraught relationship of the two most prominent families on the island, the Hookers and the Downs. They have been allies and adversaries for as long as anyone can remember. She pulls out a photo album complete with black-and-white portraits of generations now past, group shots of family gatherings, and newspaper clippings.

Again, she speaks directly to the large glass window. Chance feels like he is drifting in his boat beside her as she churns against the tide of history. She notes that the two families, Hooker and Downs, were the most influential on the island, particularly during the "time of slavery." She recounts how, at one time, there was an epic eruption of the family feud.

"…the leaders of both families—the patriarchs—unable to resolve one angry, difficult moment… agreed to meet to duel with pistols on top of Mount Pleasant. This spot was neutral to both sides and closest to the Lord.

"The day came. Papa Hooker, my great-great-grandfather, went to the Mount. He was accompanied only by a brother who carried weapons for the duel. But, as they passed through the final thicket, they were stopped. A group of men, all from the family Downs, met them before they stepped onto the storm-groomed grass atop Mount Pleasant. They surrounded the two men and killed them. This was their way of ending the dispute. It was no duel. This was murder."

A shadow falls across Miss Alva's face. Her dimpled chin points to the sea. She is motionless and silent. Again, Chance sees a living human strike the pose of a determined figurehead on a ship's prow, perhaps on a voyage of retribution or vengeance.

"My family moved to the mainland. To Bluefields. The Hooker family grew and prospered there. We produced lawyers and doctors; one studied in France, at the Sorbonne. I was the first born in my family and taught many things at school and to my family. It is why I am a teacher today. But my brother..."

She points to a portrait, and, for a moment, looks away from the open window and examines the black-and-white photo of a young man in a three-piece suit.

"My brother Waldo Wyman Hooker became a great lawyer and a leader. He brought us back to the island. He found ways to reclaim our lands. We are now friends with all people of the island, even the Downs. However, history has its way. It repeats. Repeatedly. More tea?"

Chance declines, then asks, "And what do you think of the current *Presidente*?"

"He is another in a long line of pirates. No more. No less. And his end will be the same."

The room is now nearly dark.

"Miss Alva, did you know that my name is also Hooker?"

"Yes. I know. It is why I tell you this story."

Chance thanks Miss Alva for her time and departs. Back on

the sandy road, he heads back toward Nelly's for one more night. The sea is deathly calm here on the north end, around on the leeward side of the island. There is barely any wake and next to no onshore breeze. In the stillness, he feels the cool air from the thick foliage of the forest. As he walks, he smells the perfume of ripe bananas mixed with the pungent smell of fresh horseshit on the road.

He picks up a recently fallen coconut from the road. This could be all the dinner he needs. Ahead, a man on a slump-backed horse plods his way. He sits in a long, sagging square-cut leather saddle. The man has a pair of the droopiest, saddest eyes Chance has ever seen and a long, sharp machete at his side. In an unintelligible spatter of Spanish/Creole, the horseman demands Chance give back the coconut he had just found. Chance quickly concedes and hands the "coco" to the farmer. Miss Alva's lesson of how disputes are sometimes resolved on the island is fresh in his memory.

So much for his dinner of coconut.

A CROWDED
BOAT

F or probably the last time, Chance lies on his back in the dark, just before dawn, at Nelly's shack. He listens to the now-familiar nighttime sounds: palms rustling, birds cackling, jungle brush thrashing, insistent waves crashing on the shore.

It is his day of departure from Corn Island. He is always excited by travel but is also nervous as he thinks about the unknowns that lie ahead: crossing the open Caribbean on *Nereida* with an unfamiliar crew, finding another boat to take him from Bluffton to Bluefields, then retracing his passage to Rama back up the Río Escondido. Then on to Managua and beyond.

In Rama, he will regroup and hopefully reacquaint himself with Esther, perhaps through her young boys. Right now, he feels like a young boy himself.

For the first time in months, he will be alone. And his Spanish-speaking skills have not developed as he hoped. He has limited financial means, and many recent events have not been reassuring. He takes one last bucket shower by moonlight and commits to leaving the shack at first light. He fights off uncertainty with activity by packing and repacking a small duffle bag with his last essential items. He agonizes over the possibility of missing the early departure of Nereida but comforts himself that the skipper will need daylight to clear the dock and set his course for the mainland.

Chance arrives at Little Corn dock by starlight, thanking Orion once again for showing him the way. He makes out the Nereida's silhouette sitting quiet and dark, moored to pylons, which sway with the incoming tide. He drops his bag at the end of the dock and sits beside it, watching brilliant stars fade from the sky. He is comforted by the syncopated slap of water against Nereida's hull and dozes off.

Dock planks rumble beneath him. He jerks himself awake. Two men approach, rolling a cart filled with boxes and sacks of rice, and stop beside Nereida. They are squat with sturdy shoulders and share the features of islanders whose families have been on the Corns for generations.

Chance greets them and asks, "Is Cap on board?"

They say no.

"Are you crew for the boat?"

"No."

"Traveling to the mainland?" They shake their heads.

Chance is out of questions. He thanks them and goes back to his perch at the edge of the pier. They stow their load in the hold and depart.

After a while, Chance sees Nereida's "Cap" approaching from the beach using the splayed side-to-side stride of a lifelong seaman. Sunbaked sand seems not to bother his bare feet a bit, nor the hot planks on the dock. He walks without looking down, studying cloud formations at sea. Chance has trouble suppressing an excited greeting as Cap runs his hand along the prow of the nodding Nereida, like a jockey saying "good morning" to a prized steed at the starting gate on race day.

"Buenos dias, Cap."

"Morning, Mistah. Hope you didn't spend the night here."

"Naw. Wanted to be sure not to miss you. Still heading to the Main today?"

Cap sizes up Chance as if it's the first time he's seen him. He strokes his broad chin where no whiskers grow, hikes up his shorts, and inhales a deep draft of morning sea air.

"That's still the plan. But tonight. Thought I told you not till the full tide... about dark."

"Just wanted to make sure not to miss you. Can I throw my bag on board?"

"That's all you got? Here. Give it to me. I'll put it up on the bridge. Nobody'll bother it there. We still have a bit of cargo to load."

"Yeah. I saw your crew. They've already been here."

"Got a bit more. One load won't get here until the afternoon. Why don't you go take it easy in town?"

"OK. Think I will. What about your 30 cords?"

"Pay me later. You look like you're good for it."

"When should I come back?"

"Looking to shove off about seven. Don't get the pukes, do you?"

"Not usually."

"Talk to the Chinaman. He's got just what you need."

He grabs Chance's bag and disappears below. Alone, once again, Chance critically examines the craft that will carry him back to the mainland and life as he once knew it.

Nereida is thirty-six feet long and made of wood; it appears relatively well maintained. The hull is white, and its bottom, which rises about a foot above the waterline, is painted a deep, rusty red. Thick, braided rope secures the prow and stern to the dock. There is a sizable winch on the foredeck near a hold leading to the forward compartment. A compact cabin with small windows is tucked in just behind the prow, peeking above the deck. The covered bridge with classic ship wheel and throttle provides an elevated seat for the skipper. A narrow smokestack pops through the bridge's roof, and the rear deck is open with a fabric roof supported by strong metal rods. Beneath the deck lies the ship's engine. There is a classic working-class look about the boat. It could be the *African Queen*'s younger, bigger brother.

With his bag on board and Cap busy below, Chance feels he can relax. He heads to the post office for one last visit and connection with the land-based world. He posts letters to two friends back home and picks up three addressed to him. One, from his sister, talks about her life at school in Virginia and ends by wishing him well.

Another letter, dated two weeks before, comes from a banker. The note curtly informs him that in his best interest, he as financial advisor (and old friend of the family) has stepped in and exercised authority to pay off an overloaded credit account with funds from savings certificates in Chance's name. He has operated following a procedure agreed upon "in written form" on a document signed by both before Chance's current "adventure." Despite the apparent scolding inherent in the note, Chance is relieved to see he has a comfortable credit balance in his account.

The third is written in a familiar, feminine scrawl. It comes from Mandy, praising him for his courage. He sits beneath a shady tree and reads it twice. Finishing the second reading leaves Chance feeling empty inside.

Dave heaps mango jelly onto a fluffy tortilla as he sits alone on the porch of Hotel Playa Coca. He studies a week-old issue of *La Prensa*, the Nicaraguan national paper. A server in a bright white guayabera shirt refills his cup with coffee the color of tar. Dave thanks him without looking up.

"De nada" comes the response.

However, the voice is not that of the server. It belongs to Chance, who saw Dave from the street and is now standing beside him. Dave is only slightly surprised as he folds the paper and puts it down. Chance sits and waves at the server, who brings another cup.

"Any news in that paper? Anything I need to know?"

"Thought you had gone. Didn't change your mind, did you?"

"No such luck. Leaving tonight."

"Saw all your gear was gone."

"It's already on the boat. Wanted to make sure *Nereida* didn't leave without me. Anything important in the paper?"

Local news is something the soon-to-be separated partners can always talk about. Chance's imminent departure is still a raw topic, so he's eager to discuss something, anything, else. Dave reaches for the creased copy of *La Prensa* and hands it to Chance.

A giant photo of grinning men with beards in berets and military fatigues dominates the front page. The headline reads, "Castro Embraces Kidnappers." The story recounts details of the Christmas hostage-taking in Managua. Three security guards were killed, and the guerrilla commandos prevailed. After several days of tense negotiation, *El Presidente* paid $1 million for the lives of the hostages, including members of his own family and senior government officials. The terms of the release also include safe passage of the commandos to Cuba and the freedom of fourteen imprisoned Sandinista leaders.

"So this was the thing we heard about right when we got here. We were in Managua. That's where it happened?!"

"Yeah. That's where it happened. Just before we got here."

Dave's breakfast arrives. Chance orders the same.

"So...? Sounds like a big deal. Shaking hands with Castro. What does it all mean?"

"The rebels, the Sandinistas, are back in business."

"Thought they had gone away."

"They've been up to no good for a long time."

"Three people got killed... at a Christmas party. There were Americans there."

"Yeah. A kid our age. From Maryland, if you can believe that. And just before the shooting started, the paper says the U.S. ambassador was there. And probably other bigwigs. They all left just in time."

"That was lucky."

"Maybe not just luck. Somebody probably tipped the ambo's hand. Says here he left thirty minutes before the attack began. That's not luck. That's complicity. Looks to me like the U.S. is putting its money on the Sandinistas. Castro and the White House? This soon? Strange bedfellows."

The story feels unreal, made up. Like something out of a movie. Way above Chance's head. Dave takes the news in stride and digests details like part of his breakfast. Chance washes it all down with a tall glass of mango juice.

The two erstwhile fishing partners leave international politics inside on the Hotel Playa Coca front porch with their dirty dishes. Each has a more immediate mission, and it is another brilliant Caribbean workday.

"You spoke with the skipper of your boat?"

"Yep. Imagine... calls himself 'Cap.'"

"Easy to remember."

"And a gentle reminder to the crew."

Dave stretches and looks north toward the "Grotto." Chance looks east, where open water crashes against the sand. They

198

hear engines coming from the airport, unusual for a Monday morning.

"You hear a plane?"

"Yeah. maybe more than one. Wanna go see it? I'm heading that way, back to the 'Grotto' to build more traps. You can help if you want to kill some time."

"Well... think I'll squeeze in one last swim instead of cutting my fingers on traps. Thanks anyway."

Approaching the airfield, they see that the three government planes that arrived the week before carrying *El Presidente*'s family are lined up, ready to depart. One airstrip is surrounded by armored vehicles and scores of men in fatigues, ball caps, berets, and cartridge belts. Each man in uniform carries a weapon in the ready position.

In two or three minutes at most, an armored vehicle they have not seen before pulls up directly in front of Dave and Chance. Armed soldiers, weapons directed their way, step out and assemble before them. An officer with no gun waves the gringos away.

They walk to the sandy road without looking back. Soon, one plane accelerates its engine and lifts off and then, in rapid succession, the other two follow. Dave and Chance are the only ones to be seen on the road.

Before separating, they agree to meet "mid-afternoon" for a late lunch at the Fishin' Hole. Chance tightens his knapsack to his shoulder and heads inland. Once more, he walks by the island cemetery and pauses to tell young Mike Dean goodbye. He pushes on for a trip up Mount Pleasant.

At the top of the Mount, all of Corn Island lies before him. He turns 360 degrees and takes it all in. There is lush vegetation nearby. Several worn footpaths and a road rise to where he stands, going to different corners of Corn. The Caribbean glimmers a brilliant turquoise with wild patches of greens and blues of every hue merging on the horizon beneath flotillas of cloud sweeping past delicate veils of the pale, silky, and transparent sky.

Near shore, foamy waves look like something refreshing to eat. To the north, he sees Little Corn Island and barely makes out the lighthouse there. Closer by, he observes *El Presidente*'s compound. Dark forms move around its perimeter.

It's been weeks since he's been here, having climbed the Mount on one of his earliest walks. At that time, he understood little about the island, its people, history, traditions. And he realizes he knew much less about himself. He promises to remember this view forever and takes pictures on his Minolta to preserve the moment.

He descends the windward side of the island and passes the bright red radio tower crowded with dishes and transmitters. It is the same observation point from which pirates once guarded treasure and U.S. sentinels alerted forces during wartime with "peaceful" surveillance.

Coming through the jungle, Chance bathes in fragrances of foliage and fruit. Every sense in his body reaches out to absorb the essence of Corn Island.

He trots downhill to Long Bay. Here, the *Vía Principal* is blocked with a tall chain-link fence near its northern end. A large, formal sign on the high stucco wall declares, "Propiedad Privada. No Hay Entrada" above a bold impression of Nicaragua's national seal.

Curiosity gets the best of Chance. He walks over to the iron gate and peers in. There is nothing to be seen other than a well-groomed road and thick jungle neatly trimmed back from the wall. He hears scratchy voices speaking Spanish on a radio. Then a man in a uniform like the ones he saw at the airport is suddenly in front of him. The guard sports the same beret and sunglasses Chance saw before. There is a stripe on the sleeve of the arm where an automatic weapon hangs. The radio crackles again.

"What do you want here?" asks the soldier in precise, accented English.

"I want nothing. Just here on a walk. Going to the beach." Chance points to the surf through the trees to his right.

The soldier behind the fence gives Chance a critical look. He speaks into a large handheld radio. There is a pause followed by an unintelligible response.

"No one is to come here. *Es privado aquí.* It is private. You must leave." He waves his weapon toward the open road.

"OK. OK. I mean no harm. Just on a little walk."

He smiles and turns back toward the road. Again, he hears the crackle of the soldier's radio. There is a back-and-forth exchange.

"*Detener. Regresar. Regresar!*"

The soldier's voice is now sharp, like a command.

"Gringo… come back. Stop. Come back!"

Something in the soldier's tone is alarming. Chance would probably run, if it weren't for the automatic weapon pointing at his back. He returns to the fence.

"You told me to go. I'm going. Like you said."

"Show me your paper. Where is your paper?"

"Paper? What paper?"

"Paper. *Pasaporte! Dame tu pasaporte. Prisa. Prisa.*"

Suddenly, Chance feels like he's been pulled over for a speeding ticket—or worse. There's no blue light: just a man behind a fence with a beret with two hands on an automatic weapon. He moves slowly toward the fence and instinctively pats the valuables pouch beneath his shirt. He's comforted by the feel of his wallet and passport there.

Then he has a sickening feeling.

This is the fifth week he and Dave have been on Corn Island. During the logistics discussion brought on by Chance's imminent departure, the two travelers discussed visas. Dave, having come from nearby Jamaica, did not need one. Being a

Caribbean neighbor, there is no limit to how long he can stay in Nicaragua.

Chance, on the other hand, comes from the States. He was issued a visa for just thirty days, and it has now expired. Fear creeps up from the core of his belly. He saunters back toward the fence.

Now the soldier leans in. His beret presses against the fence. The muzzle of his weapon points through the steel bars in Chance's direction.

"*Prisa*. Bring me your paper, gringo. Show your passport. I must see it, now!"

Chance moves slowly as his mind races through his options. He has seen many firearms in his life, but this is the first that has ever been pointed in his direction. He pats his pockets as though looking for the passport hanging unseen in its pouch beneath his armpit. He sees no other option than doing as the armed guard says. He unbuttons his shirt.

The soldier's radio erupts in staticky chatter, which for a moment he ignores. Then a second voice takes over the radio feed. It is sharper, more emphatic. The soldier steps back from the fence and lets his weapon dangle from his shoulder. Chance fingers the passport in his pouch.

Now the soldier turns his back and walks away from the fence. He listens intently to orders being issued on the radio. He continues to walk away, saying nothing. The exchange ends and the soldier clips the radio to his belt. Assuming the "ready" position with his automatic weapon, he turns and starts back toward the fence.

Chance is gone.

The soldier fires three quick rounds into the air.

Chance runs through the surf, holding his work boots under one arm, slowing down only when he reaches Long Bay. He has never run so fast, so far.

He thinks back to when he was a boy on the Georgia coast. He learned to love "the beach" with all its secrets and treasures at a very young age. However, there, the water was murky and dark. Here the sea is clean, clear, and shines like a jewel. He feels spoiled and wonders if this is the most beautiful water in the world. He challenges himself to travel more and find out.

In his mind, Chance has already left Corn Island. He spends the day discreetly swimming at a familiar spot on Long Bay. Enormous fleets of small fish wander above the coral reefs. Barracuda and nurse sharks also swim by. Chance takes a dip in the water now and then knowing he may never have this view again. Feeling anxious and alone, he jots notes in his diary and steels himself for the solo journey ahead.

Back at the Fishin' Hole, the one place on the island he feels fairly safe, Chance treats himself to an early beer and waits for Dave's arrival for a final bite together. While restocking the bar, owner Lyle agrees to cash a traveler's check, a favor this early in the week, long before the "bank" arrives by air on Friday.

After a while, J #1 and J #2 gather at a table with a couple of new faces dressed just as they are. Chance orders a second beer.

Trapper Jack comes in and sits at his usual spot. Soon, a young lady sits at Jack's table, then another, and another. A beer arrives in front of Chance. Lyle tells him, "Compliments of the Jamaican." Chance gives his trap-building mentor a raised bottle salute. Jack returns the gesture but quickly redirects his full attention to courting the young ladies, who are all outfitted in brief shorts and colorful tops.

Henri arrives and finds a discreet table near the back. Chance returns a wave the quiet, dark seaman sends his way. Soon, Henri's table fills with his brothers. This is the first time Chance has seen Henri and cohorts at the Fishin' Hole. It seems early in the day for so much traffic here.

Henri and brothers crowd around the jukebox. Familiar reggae tunes fill the Hole and Lyle places another foaming lager before Chance. He feels something strange in the air.

Now Dave enters the bar with a package in hand and Pansy at his side. Two men from the crowd at the jukebox bring a table to the center of the room. Space is cleared for it. Dave places his load on the table. It remains covered.

Lyle places yet another lager before Chance. This one has a shot glass beside it.

"Compliments of Henri and the brothers."

Other familiar faces fill the Hole.

"I didn't know this place filled up so early. Particularly on a Monday."

"It usually doesn't. I guess today's a little special."

Trays are brought from the kitchen—compliments of Don Dean—who are not there. Dave stands in the middle of the noisy crowd.

"Listen up," yells Lyle, who looks over to Dave. Dave nods.

Lyle blows three loud notes on a boatswain's whistle that he keeps behind the bar. All eyes go his way and he gestures toward Dave. Lyle blows the whistle again. Henri looks to turn down the volume on the jukebox, finds no switch, and pulls the plug out of the wall. The bar falls quiet.

"Mister Dave has something to say."

"Just a brief word, thank you, Mister Lyle."

Dave steps away from the food-laden table to the center of the Hole's tiny dance floor. Chance immediately recognizes Dave's white dinner jacket with frayed cuffs and realizes that "something's up." Dave smiles shyly into the crowd, then looks to the floor, where he seems to study words written there.

"This will be brief. First, I wish to thank you all for sharing your island. I have never felt more at home than here on Corn.

Even with family back in Jamaica, I never felt so welcome as here.

"My partner Mister Chance is leaving us today. I hope to see him again soon. We have shared many struggles. And... it has not always been easy between us."

Chance raises a glass and nods from the bar. Dave looks directly toward him.

"I have here a small memento of our time together and a reminder of how valuable it has been to me. I hope you use it well. Please join me in a toast to my partner... my companion, my friend.

"Fair winds, Mister Chance. And following seas." They salute each other with single-gulp shots.

Everyone in the room raises a drink of some sort; even Lyle behind the bar pours a stiff one and knocks it back in one gulp. The room echoes with salutes to Chance as Dave hands his partner an ornate knife about eight inches long. Chance is too surprised to speak. He raises his re-filled shot glass, salutes the room, and gives Dave as manly a hug around the shoulders as he can muster.

"Now for the real important words: let's eat!"

Dave pulls back a cloth at the table in the center of the room. There are platters piled with boiled shrimp and fried plantain. And there is a large basin filled with Rundown. Dave serves up the stew in cups and bowls. Everyone consumes the fare with the ceremony and satisfaction they would share over egg nog at midnight on New Year's Eve.

Enthused by the proceedings and luxuriating in a full bar this early in the day, owner Lyle comps Chance's standing tab. Moved by the experience and Lyle's generosity, Chance leaves a worn U.S. five-dollar bill on the counter.

The food disappears in minutes. And when the final creamy cups of Corn Island Rundown are gone, Dave's one-time partner is nowhere to be seen.

When Chance arrives at Little Corn dock, he is relieved to see slow activity on *Nereida*. A stoop-shouldered man Chance has not seen before moves around the ship's decks. High tide marks on the sand and watermarks on moorings indicate that it is still about two hours before full tide. That makes it roughly 5 p.m. He is eager to depart but knows it will be a while.

The setting sun paints the sky the color of salmon, then peach, and soon hibiscus as it sinks toward the sea. Finally, the sun drops beneath the horizon like a hot tangerine. Chance wonders why there's so little movement on the *Nereida*. He walks over and shouts up to the one hand on board.

"Hola! G'wan? Hello?"

"Hello, Suh."

"Speak English?"

"I say yes. Some say No."

The stoop-shouldered man stops what he's doing and leans on a mop. Protruding cheeks beneath nearly closed eyes shine as brightly as his bald head in the angled light. He smiles from ear to ear, but his face seems compressed. Chance guesses he has no teeth.

"Is the ship moving out soon? Tide looks like it's getting high to me."

"Up to the Cap. I'm just the mate. You must be the passenger he told me about. I'm clearing space for you now."

"Yeah. Cap here? Said he'd leave about seven. Must be near that."

"Might be. But Cap's not here. Told me to get everything set to go. Leaving a bit later than we thought. Waiting for a few more to board. But tonight for sure."

Chance takes this news like a punch in the gut.

"Not what he told me this morning."

"Yeah. Got some more riders. They're coming from 'cross the island. Will take some time to get here. Come on board if you like. Deck's all clear. You can set up your berth." Mate's broad grin confirms he's toothless."

Stowing his disappointment like unwanted baggage, Chance gathers his pack and boards the boat. There's plenty of room. There's nothing on the rear deck except canvas awning about eight feet high, held in place with pipes secured directly to the deck. There's easy passage to the bow on each side of the bridge. High gunwales up to Chance's hips should keep down the sea spray. And the smokestack funnel rising from the bridge is tall, so there should be no problem with smoke.

He asks for permission to go below and visit the head. There's a mini galley at the foot of the ladder and four small bunks. The cabin is crowded with life jackets, cooking utensils, and nautical gear. Voices crackle over a radio at a compact navigation station across from the head.

Back in the open, Chance picks a spot near the stern to stow his stuff.

"Think you'll like it better here, Mistah," says Mate. He points to a deep, wide bench above a locker just behind the bridge. He opens it to reveal fishing rods, tools, and a long rope with floats.

Chance begins to arrange his gear by the bench; he unrolls a hammock, mounts one end to a cleat on the rail, and looks for another cleat to draw it tight.

"We better get you higher. You won't be the only one on board."

Chance thinks back to previous trips on boats in Nicaragua. He remembers the crowded downstream cruise from Rama to Bluefields on the Río Escondido, bumpy passage across a sound to El Bluff, being soaked with sea spray and bitter despair on deck of the *Max 5* from the mainland to Corn Island. Three different trips, three sets of turbulent conditions. During six uncertain weeks in Central America, he has learned to listen to locals.

Now his latest advisor, the toothless Mate, helps Chance string his hammock directly to vertical supports holding up the rear awning. He ties clove hitch knots around horizontal pipes high above the deck. Chance thinks the hammock is hanging too high, but his new shipmate assures him that "as high as possible is best." Together, they stow the gringo's travel bag in the on-deck locker with a waterproof lid.

As they work together, Mate speaks about his life on land and sea. He grew up in a big family in Louisiana that "worked the fields... with so much family I never knew all the names." He learned English and Creole from an early age, "...calling brothers cousins and cousins brothers, loving them all the same." He is among the youngest of many brothers, who were tended by sisters who acted like mothers. At fourteen, he traveled to the port of New Orleans because it was "... front door to the whole world."

"Now I am a 'Salt' for life, and everyone calls me Mate."

It's a tricky climb into his bunk, but it's oddly comfortable once Chance settles in. Only his valuables pouch, waterproof jacket, food bag, book, and flashlight join him aloft. Adjusting like a caterpillar in a cocoon, he reads for a minute or two, then falls deeply asleep as dusk turns to dark.

The creaking of mooring cables soothes Chance's sleep for a few hours. Then, abruptly, a cacophony of noise forces him to wake.

A noisy truck renders shouting voices unintelligible. Shrill animal squeals pierce the quiet night. Chance recognizes the "thump, thump" of bare feet moving down the dock. The thumps are emphatic and determined. There are more high-pitched squeals, and multiple voices compete for attention.

Chance climbs awkwardly from his cozy nest. He looks around the bridge, across the main deck, out to sea, searching for the source of the ear-piercing squealing and guttural grunting.

Taillights and brake lights from a large pickup cast a glow on the dock. Flashlight beams scan the *Nereida*, choppy water, and each other as they compete for attention, leading the truck down the pier. There are shouts of warning and encouragement.

The truck driver leans out his window and creeps the truck cautiously toward *Nereida*. There is very little room between the truck and the choppy bay. Sharp squealing from the rear of the truck rises in volume and escalates in frequency.

Now wide-awake and slightly confused, Chance watches from *Nereida* 's foredeck. Cap leans out a window on the bridge and shouts to Mate, who, leading the noisy procession on the dock, shines his light in Cap's eyes while calling something back. Neither hears the other. The gringo passenger feels like he's watching a movie, something comic like *The Three Stooges,* or maybe a Disney cartoon.

The pickup pulls parallel to *Nereida* and stops. The cargo bed is walled with warped plywood about five feet high, completely concealing its contents. Chance has seen many trucks like this on the island and in Central America, usually crammed with men shoulder to shoulder on their way to work. There appears to be no human in the bed, but it is a busy mass of motion, making lots of noise.

Mate steps onto the boat and drops its ramp to the dock. The two dockhands, "Pete and Repeat," suddenly appear and climb into the truck bed. Mate, now standing at the rear of the truck, cautiously removes a narrow plywood panel. The head of a giant pig pops out. Two others struggle to occupy the same space but can only force their snouts to the open air.

Chance watches as Mate and helpers remove eight enormous pigs from the truck and, using short ropes, lead them one by one onto the boat. The pigs are large, about the size of starting varsity linemen. They are not in the least cooperative. It takes three workers to move one pig from truck to boat and then tie it to a steel stanchion. The squealing protests from the pigs are now even louder than before. They take up all the open space on the boat deck. As soon as the truck's cargo bed is empty, it races away from the dock.

Mate stays on the *Nereida* deck, securing each pig in place.

"What's going on here?" shouts Chance, leaning under the deck canvas roof.

"Should be shoving off soon," Mate yells back.

"What's with the animals?"

"Told you there'd be other passengers."

"These aren't passengers. They're pigs!"

"Oh. They'll settle down once we head out."

"The pigs will go to sleep? How far are they going?"

"They'll settle down. Not that far to Rama, they'll be gone by breakfast."

"That's a lot of bacon." Chance can barely make out what Mate is saying between the grunts and squeals.

"Won't be long now. Here comes the last load."

Chance stands beside Mate and watches another truck back down the dark dock. He knows something about weight loads on small vessels and so is appalled when he sees that this truck is also loaded with pigs.

"Where will you put these pigs? The boat is already full. There's nowhere for them to go."

"Don't worry, my friend," says Mate, now grinning, "we will make it work. We always do. Found room for you, didn't we?"

Eight more pigs are led on board. Chance counts sixteen enormous, snotty snouts as the second truck pulls away. The *Nereida* now rides lower in the water. The noise from this living load of sausage, chops, and tripe is deafening. Chance crawls inside his hammock. He can only hope for the best.

In minutes, *Nereida* pulls away from the dock. Chance sees smoke billowing from the smokestack but cannot hear the engine chugging to fight the chop. He hopes *Nereida*'s motion on the open water will somehow soothe the huge beasts squirming and nudging bare inches from his backside. However, when they are fully underway, the noisy complaints from his fellow porky passengers grow even louder in the pitching sea.

The sounds, discomfort, and indignity of the entire experience are so horrible that Chance can only laugh. He lies, body clenched, hammock swinging and sinking toward sixteen drooling snouts. Looking up at the clear night sky, he searches for constellations to erase the image of this comic departure from Corn Island from his mind.

As he looks to the stars for solace, he suddenly remembers it's February 14, Valentine's Day.

FLOATING
UPSTREAM

The *Nereida* leaves Little Corn dock around midnight, riding low in the water with a full load: sixteen angry pigs, a gringo passenger suspended above them, one Mate, one Cap, and lots of rice. The tide and sea current are both against the vessel as it chugs toward the Nicaragua mainland.

It takes all night to make it to El Bluff. Chance twists in his hammock to relieve the strain on his back but can barely move. With each turn or minimal adjustment, the hammock sinks closer to the howling pigs, which are now in open rebellion and noisy combat with one another. Whenever one pig mounts on the back of another, it lasts only moments as the rocking deck pitches from side to side and the disappointed pig slams back down on all fours, raising new cries of outrage from partners below.

Chance struggles out of his hammock and stands on the elevated locker. He unties then reties the ropes on the hammock to lift it higher above the pigpen. Relying on his best tying skills, he is confident he has elevated his perch. However, there is no improvement. Lying on his back, cramped as before, he scans the Eastern horizon and sees—or imagines—dawn's early light and an end to this excruciating night.

He crawls up on the back deck and fights off nausea. As the morning sky fills with a pastel glow, Chance takes a seat on the bow. He makes out a landmass on the horizon and watches it grow as *Nereida* fights her way toward shore. A string of shrimp boats, night lights still glowing, heads his way.

He thinks about the last time he crossed these waters, with Dave. It was a moment of bright hope and abject defeat. The memory of watching his future drift away in a dugout canoe haunts Chance every day. He asks Cap if he can sit on the bridge's roof as the *Nereida* approaches shore.

"Hold on tight," the stern-faced Captain warns as they fight their way into the harbor.

Chance is relieved to reach El Bluff. Charter fishing boats head out to sea, and scrappy pangas depart with local commuters on their way to work up and down the coast. A multi-storied customs tower oversees it all. Here, at the highest open observation deck, a uniformed man with a burr haircut paces back and forth, noting arrivals, unloadings, loadings, and departures.

Nereida crosses Bahía de Bluefields and docks at Bluefields within an hour; the squirming, squealing swine are only slightly quieter than when they boarded the boat. But Chance has grown accustomed to the din.

Before they tie up, Chance's new friend Mate hands him a large cup of coffee, filling him with joy and gratitude. The warmth in his hands feels like a bounteous gift, a symbol of more than just their brief encounter. It reminds the gringo of the generosity he has experienced over and over throughout this strange trip.

"There is a little river 'chugger' called *Oh Me* ready to take you to Rama," Mate tells Chance.

"Really? How do you know?"

"I sail these waters always. I know all the boats, all the crews."

"The boat has a place for me?"

"Oh, yes. We speak with their skipper by radio. He will take you to Rama. But you must hurry on board."

Chance has no words for this thoughtful gesture. He pulls out two sizable córdoba bills from the pouch beneath his shirt and hands them to Mate.

"I thank you for everything. There are two notes here. One is for Cap and one is for you."

Mate puts the notes in his shirt pocket. Then he gathers and uncoils a pile of mooring lines from the deck while squinting at the rapidly approaching dock. He looks up at the bridge and gives the Cap a wave, then squints at Chance.

"You must hurry to catch *Oh Me*," Mate tells Chance as he tosses the line to a young hand standing on the dock.

Chance barely hears these final words over the nonstop squealing of the floating pig farm.

The early morning rhythm of the Nicaraguan waterfront is now familiar. Chance steps off the *Nereida* ahead of the pigs but must take his turn on the ramp between men unloading rice. Stepping on solid ground for the first time in many hours, he is quickly absorbed by a teeming mass of workers streaming up and down the dock. He hurries to find the boat called *Oh Me*.

The bright blue and red barge sits low in the water. It is broad-beamed and short in stature. There is no bridge or pilot-house. The boat's skipper sits on a tall seat at the fore of the long and expansive deck. A low, open roof covers two rows of bench seats. There is a tiny cabin beneath the foredeck containing the boat's engine and one crude WC.

Chance pays fifteen córdobas to the deckhand for passage to Rama. The barge will leave soon and arrive about dark. He left Corn Island about midnight the night before and calculates he has traveled roughly eighty miles in sixteen hours. That's a bit faster than he can walk and certainly worth the two or three dollars it cost.

He climbs the gangplank to *Oh Me*, walks both sides of the pews, and selects a space on the starboard side. His arrival causes a ripple effect through the passengers already seated there, who provide him with a few more inches of seating space.

The approximately 100-kilometer upriver voyage from Bluefields to Rama will take almost twice as long as the journey downstream. *Oh Me* pushes forward against a strong current, and there are many stops along the way where passengers get off and others get on with fanfare and flutter.

Chance is not surprised by the slow progress. The gringo soaks up views of lush scenery that drifts by as the boat moves upstream at a gentle pace, stopping unpredictably at thatch houses perched on riverbanks to take on more passengers, coconuts, and bananas.

Finally, they pull up to Rama. Tropical trees sway like Broadway silhouettes against a hand-painted sky. Two boisterous men board the boat before the gangplank is put in place. Chance cobbles together their loud message telling those on board that a "...bus for Managua departs at 3 a.m."

Chance groans at this news. The bus will be his ride to Managua to begin his trip back home, but from the look of the sky, it's probably not even 8 p.m.

Chance heads to the Hotel Del Rio. The path there reminds him of his first visit a few weeks before, which now seems like ages ago. He has experienced much since then and has changed. Even his loping gait is different: more confident, honed by experiences that would previously have been unimaginable.

Maybe he can just nap on the porch.

ONE SPECIAL NIGHT

C hance steps quickly across the hotel porch and finds the owner at the front desk, looking like he was expecting him. Chance's body sags with relief. The notion of a private chamber, a bed with a mattress, clean sheets, and no squealing pigs seems like heaven.

Chance asks for a room and is led through the dark hall to the hand-carved door of the same room he shared with Dave. Sweet jungle fragrances wash over him when the owner opens the shuttered window. He suddenly feels very tired.

Two hours later, Chance returns to the front desk, refreshed by a bath and a nap. He pays for his room. He is now quite hungry but is not surprised to hear the kitchen is closed for the night. The hotel owner points to carts on the street where he can find good local fare.

Out on the porch, Chance looks toward the dock and discerns quiet activity. He is not inspired by the food options available. Then, at the far corner of the porch, he notices a figure sitting on a large settee, looking out at the moon-glazed jungle. It is Esther.

"Hola. Miss Esther?"

"Hello."

"Hi. I'm Chance. Chance Hooker. We met before. A couple of weeks ago."

"I remember. I thought you wouldn't see me here."

The young traveler looks out on the night and is suddenly struck dumb. He soaks in the cool evening air.

"This is my favorite time. It is like this here every evening."

"How are your boys?"

"They are themselves."

"It would be fun to see them again."

"They are with their *tío* tonight. Upriver. In Esperanza. They will return tomorrow."

He moves closer along the front porch rail, to hear her better.

"I guess I'll have to catch them next time I'm here. I'm leaving tonight—well, very early in the morning—on the bus to Managua. Then back to the States."

"They will miss seeing you. You and your partner made quite an impression."

"Hope I'm not interrupting."

"Not at all."

Chance leans against a post, looking back to where Esther sits. She glows in the single electric porch light, long dark hair pulled back in a bun, shapely torso, and slender athletic legs crossed at the ankle, resting on the rail. She looks confident and totally at home.

"Your trip was a success? I am surprised to see you back here so soon."

Chance recounts his stay on Corn Island. It is the first time he has put the experience into words. He describes the loss of the dugout purchased from *Tío* on the open water. He talks about building traps, successful dives, and the death of Mike Dean. He mostly speaks about the people of Corn Island: their warmth, hospitality, and acceptance of two young travelers. Then he stops, noticing his monologue has gone on for several minutes.

"Sorry. Got carried away."

"No problem. I wondered. Almost every day."

Chance hears the breeze in the trees and feels content. For a moment, he imagines living a quiet life here in Rama. Then his stomach grumbles. Esther smothers a motherly laugh.

"Hungry?"

"Starved. I was just heading out to visit one of those carts on the wharf. Will you join me?"

"You don't want anything from those carts at this time of night. Trust me."

"Well... the kitchen is closed here."

"I know. But some residents have certain privileges."

He looks at her slim silhouette against the backdrop of moon-glazed foliage. The wharf seems very far away.

"Come with me," says Esther, rising from her seat and heading indoors.

They walk through the quiet lobby, past the unmanned front desk. They enter a pantry jammed with painted plates, bowls, and cups. A narrow table is contained on one wall by two high-backed benches facing each other, creating a private booth. Above the table, a little window glows, spilling light across the glossy tabletop. The dimly lit kitchen waits just beyond the pantry.

"Have a seat here," Esther says, disappearing into the kitchen.

Chance slides into the booth, unsure whether he's being treated like a guest or one of her boys. There's a casual orderliness about the pantry. It reminds him of the diner back home where Dave first presented the idea of traveling to Nicaragua.

Chance now feels at home in this country, which only two months before felt impossibly foreign.

He marvels at the way that the moon glowing in the sky right now is the same here in Rama as over Virginia's Blue Ridge Mountains. He relishes the way he is sharing this moment here and now with only one other person.

Esther returns with a small tray. She places two cocktail glasses with ice on the table. Beside them, she puts a tall bottle of rum with a fancy label, limes cut in quarters, and a pitcher filled with mango juice. She pours two strong shots.

"Some say it's the best Jamaica has to offer. I don't know. I certainly haven't tried them all. Mango on top?"

Chance appreciates the certainty in her voice as well as her large dark eyes, arched eyebrows, and softly pronounced features.

"Yes. Thanks."

Right now, they are the only two people on the planet, and he likes it that way. They have a drink, then two. Chance is amazed at how relaxed he feels sitting opposite this square-shouldered woman.

"So why did you leave so soon? Did you have a falling out?"

"Well, we were running out of money, but that was not the main reason. Dave and I are on two different tracks. He's an artist who wants to be a businessman. I'm a handcrafter who wants to be an artist. Back home in Virginia, I'm restoring an old, historic building from the ground up. Using money left me by my grandparents, I bought a pile of bricks instead of a Corvette. But, really, what I am is a bit of a storyteller. So don't get me started."

"I have time," Esther says, refilling his glass. "You're the one on a schedule. Ready for dinner?"

"Almost always."

There is seriousness in her voice but not in her dark, liquid eyes. Her eyebrows arch high, and her cheekbones and jaw stand out sharply. There is a hint of crimson on her lips above a pointed, dimpled chin.

Chance joins Esther in the kitchen, where the double doors with glass panes open onto a small, empty yard just before the jungle. She lights two oil lamps flanking a propane stove and goes straight to work, preparing pork steaks and French toast. As skillets sizzle on the stove, Esther sets a lavish table for one at the pantry booth. Chance sits. She retreats once more to the kitchen.

"Can I help?"

"Stay put. You look a little beat."

Esther returns with a mountain of food. Chance devours the meal while she tells him more about her family life before she came to Rama. She pours fresh drinks from the pitcher, this time mixing a little less rum, and pushes one forward to Chance.

"This will fill your soul, they say, and open your heart."

"It also opens your mouth. I haven't stopped talking since we sat down."

"I don't mind."

"Take a walk?"

"I'd like that."

They step down to the sandy lane, where there's no one else around. Even the distant wharf is uncommonly quiet. Chance finds he is holding her hand. It is warm, compliant.

"How long have you been here?"

"We came five years ago to build the family. But it didn't work out. He had other plans—a big practice in the States. I stayed. I don't blame him. He left me with the two greatest treasures on Earth."

"There's no one else?"

"I don't have time. Maybe someday."

They head back to the hotel, step up to the porch where they met weeks earlier, and enter the lobby. They are the only ones there.

"Wake up."

Chance lies still, knowing the voice is from a dream.

"Wake up," he hears once again, this time feeling a hand shake his shoulder.

Chance rolls over and sees Esther's deep, dark eyes probing his, lit by a small lamp across the room. She smiles and goes limp in his arms.

"You must get up. The bus to Managua will leave in less than an hour."

"Have you seen it? Is it here?" Chance asks, suddenly alarmed.

"No. You will know when it arrives. It is loud."

He holds her close.

"Thank you for this. Thank you for everything."

"It was meant to be."

Again, they sit on the porch. This time, they hold hands on the settee. The sound of a vehicle faintly penetrates rustling palms. The sound grows more insistent. Soon, headlamps are visible in the distance. They bob up and down and rock side to side. A piercing voice sings out. Its volume increases rapidly.

"Managua! Managua! Managua!"

As the bus passes the hotel, Chance is surprised to see that it is a well-maintained Mercedes. The bus pulls up to the wharf, where a young man leans out the front door, shouting once again, "Managua! Managua! Managua."

"You must go. The bus will not stay here long. Only minutes. You will be in Managua before lunch."

"I will be back."

"I know," Esther says, not believing it.

Esther walks Chance to the commercial dock, which he has grown to know so well. It is 3 a.m. and looks quite different now. Only one other passenger stands waiting to board the bus, a man with a bulging, woven bag wrapped with cord, wearing a sombrero with a tightly curled brim.

Chance waves at Esther from a seat at the rear of the bus as it pulls away. She also waves, holding a shawl drawn tightly around her shoulders.

The gringo doubts he will ever see her again.

WELCOME BACK, ROOKIE

The bus from Rama back to Managua moves no faster than the diesel-powered commuter boat struggling upstream on the Río Escondido. Every stop of the comfortable Mercedes shuttle is preceded by hair-raising horn blasts and shouts of "Managua! Managua! Managua!" from a skinny ticket taker leaning out the door.

He arrives in Nicaragua's capital late morning; there are more uniformed men than before carrying loaded automatic weapons. They direct traffic at corners and patrol the streets in squads. Pedestrians move quickly, their heads turned down. He senses reprisal and revolution in the air.

The young American has learned a great deal about Central America in the past two months, particularly about its autocratic suppression and social upheaval. He is ready to return home to political stability, familiar faces, and a comfortable bed. He takes a taxi back to the Hotel Carlos V, where he recognizes *El Loro* behind the desk.

"Welcome, señor. Your compadre is parking the car?"

"*Hola, Señor Loro.* You remember me. No, this time I am alone."

"Of course I remember you, Don Hooker. This is your home in Managua."

Chance surveys the lobby, with its broken fixtures, faded paint, and buckled marble floor. Compared to Nelly's shack, it feels like a palace. He negotiates a price for a room and follows "The Parrot" back to the same one he and Dave shared before. He sleeps through the rest of the day, gets up for dinner, and then sleeps soundly all through the night.

The next day, he takes several tiny taxis around Managua's fields of rubble to find a way back home. At the airport, he learns the only affordable way is by air from San José, capital of neighboring Costa Rica. He spends several hours at the office of *Migración* and finds he needs a visa to enter Costa Rica. He has to go to the consulate across town to get one.

Here, he meets Jon Franco, another solo traveler also in pursuit of a visa for Costa Rica. Franco is Italian and making his way to Venezuela to teach there but must also fly from the States to do so. They compare itineraries and agree to join company on a drive to San José in Jon's classic AMC Rambler. Chance will help with the gas.

They leave early the next day, though they are in no particular rush. As they drive, Chance learns that Jon holds a PhD in physics and has just completed a teaching assignment at San José State University in California. They drive in a leisurely way through León and Granada and stop for a dip in Lake Nicaragua, despite knowing that freshwater sharks swim and feed there. They enter Costa Rica easily and are only mildly irritated by the scalping freelance moneychangers at the border.

Arriving in San José, Chance is struck by the Costa Rican capital's affluence. Its well-dressed people and neatly groomed roadways are a dramatic contrast to Nicaragua. He indulges himself in a room at the Plaza Hotel and an all-American dinner at McDonald's with Jon. They separate the next day at the airport.

Now Chance looks out from a window seat on a LANICA Airlines DC-3 at Cuba, which is thirty-thousand feet below. He is about an hour by air from Miami. He thinks a little about what lies ahead and a lot about what he has left behind.

The past two days have been a whirlwind, but now the brilliant Caribbean stretches ahead as he makes his way to Miami, travel gear tucked beneath his feet.

"Hm. Cuba," he says to himself. "Will I ever be able to go there?"

ACKNOWLEDGMENTS

Many people contributed to completion of this book. In particular, thanks go to Hugh Barker, whose spot on observations and firm suggestions kept the main characters engaged. I am deeply indebted to Bethany Davis, whose keen eye and gentle persuasion kept this runaway train on track. Once more, Syneca Featherstone demonstrated her uncanny ability to convert verbal communication into visual art.

And I offer eternal appreciation to Peggy Sullivan for her relentless encouragement.

ABOUT THE AUTHOR

Chip Hunter is an Emmy Award–winning writer, producer, and director. He has traveled extensively through the U.S., Canada, Mexico, Central America, Europe, and Africa. Chip has worked for numerous broadcast and cable networks and been recognized for local community service as an Olympic Torchbearer. *Corn Island Rundown* is his first novel. He has also published a memoir titled *Stage Monkey* about his early days as a backstage theatre professional.

Made in the USA
Middletown, DE
11 April 2023

28622829R00135